Exodus 20:15

The Ultimate Chocolate Cake

The Ultimate Chocolate Cake

and 110 Other Chocolate Indulgences

HELGE RUBINSTEIN

Congdon & Weed, Inc.
New York

Library of Congress Cataloging in Publication Data
Rubinstein, Helge.
The ultimate chocolate cake and 110 other
chocolate indulgences.

First published in 1982 under title: The chocolate book.
Bibliography: p.
Includes index.
1. Cookery (Chocolate) I. Title. II. Title:
Ultimate chocolate cake and one hundred ten other
chocolate indulgences.
TX767.C5R83   1983   641.6'374   83–1796
ISBN 0-86553-078-5
ISBN 0-312-92851-3 (St. Martin's Press)

Published by Congdon & Weed, Inc.
298 Fifth Avenue, New York, N.Y. 10001

Distributed by St. Martin's Press
175 Fifth Avenue, New York, N.Y. 10010

Published simultaneously in Canada by Thomas Nelson & Sons Limited
81 Curlew Drive, Don Mills, Ontario M3A 2R1

Published in Great Britain 1982 as *The Chocolate Book* by
Penguin Books Ltd

*For Chocoholics
everywhere,
those nearest and dearest
in particular*

Said to be the oldest engraving in existence on cocoa. It shows the 'mother tree' on the right shading a delicate young cocoa tree.

CONTENTS

PREFACE

Every book reflects something of its author, and cookery books are no exception. Only a devoted chocolate-lover could embark on a project which involved not merely cooking but also eating (or at least tasting) over a hundred chocolate dishes, most of them over and over again.

Happily, I am married to a self-confessed Chocoholic, and have produced a family who seemed more than content to have a chocolate dessert every day for well over a year. My own love of chocolate falls a little short of addiction, and is tinged with a certain Puritanism. I was brought up to believe that you *never* ate chocolate until after lunch, and even now am truly shocked at those of my friends who will eat chocolate cake for breakfast, and one who has been known to demolish half a box of the best chocolates before she even gets out of bed in the morning.

This book has evolved gradually. First and foremost it was to be a cookbook, with a sprinkling of quotations and anecdotes, but the more I learned, the more fascinated I became by chocolate history and lore. I hope my readers will also enjoy both aspects of the book.

Helge Rubinstein
London, 1981

7 556

INTRODUCTION

COOKING WITH CHOCOLATE

I am a purist about chocolate. I like only the best, and the best, for me, means a really dark, bittersweet or semi-sweet variety. When it comes to cooking, my taste does not change, but economic factors begin to weigh.

With chocolate, as with everything else in cooking, the better the quality of the raw material, the better the end result. If I am making a rich dessert, like a *marquise*, for a special occasion, or something very light, like a *pot au chocolat*, I will use only the finest of the dark fondant chocolates; for less special cakes or desserts, less expensive plain chocolate will do. Use the best you can afford, but whichever brand you choose, it must be *real chocolate*, and not a chocolate substitute, or one of the 'chocolate-flavoured' coatings that are sold for cooking purposes, and which are not made with chocolate liquor or cocoa butter.

UNSWEETENED CHOCOLATE

Unsweetened chocolate can be used instead of what the British call plain or bitter chocolate in most recipes, provided you adjust the amount of sugar to taste.

MILK CHOCOLATE

'Milk chocolate is a yokel taste,' says Stanley Marcus in his book, *Quest for the Best*. While not going quite that far, I have not used milk chocolate in any recipes. This is not merely a matter of personal taste, but also because the cocoa content is less, so the flavour of a finished dish made with milk chocolate will not be nearly so rich.

WHITE CHOCOLATE

White chocolate is not really chocolate at all. It consists of cocoa butter, milk and sugar, but contains no chocolate liquor; hence its colour. After numerous unsuccessful experiments, I abandoned it. The thought of producing all-white 'chocolate' dishes was amusing, but no one knew that they were chocolate until they were told.

CHOCOLATE COUVERTURE

Couverture is generally available only to professionals, so I have not specified it in any recipes. Melted, it flows more smoothly than ordinary chocolate because of its high cocoa butter content; if you can get hold of some you will find it invaluable for covering delicate cakes or chocolates.

STORING CHOCOLATE

Chocolate should be stored in a cool, dry place. Plain chocolate can be kept under such conditions for more than a year without loss of flavour; milk chocolate can be similarly stored for about six months.

It can be kept in the refrigerator or freezer, but may sweat when brought to room temperature. This 'bloom', or the slight whitish film that sometimes develops, is merely a little cocoa butter or some sugar crystals that have risen to the surface. It will not impair the flavour and disappears as soon as the chocolate is melted.

MELTING CHOCOLATE

Chocolate is temperamental and very sensitive when heated, but provided you understand the basic rules it should give you no trouble.

Chocolate melted on its own must *never* be allowed to exceed a temperature of 44°C (110°F), and it must always be kept perfectly dry.

There are several ways of melting it safely:

1   In the top of a double boiler or in a bowl set over hot water. The simplest and safest way I have found is to bring the water to the boil in the lower pan, remove it from the heat and set the container with the chocolate in it on top. In this way, there is no danger of steam touching and spoiling the chocolate. If you are melting a great quantity, you may have to reheat the water briefly.

2   In a very low oven (110°C, or 225°F maximum). This method is very slow but very safe, and fine if you are not in a hurry and the oven is on anyway. If you have a solid fuel range (a wood stove, for instance), use the warming oven.

3   I understand chocolate can be melted successfully in a microwave oven (2−3 minutes, depending on the wattage of your microwave oven and the type of chocolate) but have not had the opportunity to try this myself.

Never melt chocolate over direct heat, unless you are in a very great hurry and prepared to watch it like a hawk.

If by chance the chocolate overheats and stiffens, it can usually be salvaged by stirring in some vegetable shortening (*not* butter, which contains too much moisture).

While chocolate will 'seize' immediately if it comes into contact with the slightest moisture when being melted alone, it is perfectly all right to melt it in a small amount of liquid (not less than 1 tablespoon). Where the recipe calls for this, put the chocolate and liquid in the bowl together;

they will blend perfectly when stirred. Chocolate may also be added to a large quantity of hot liquid, but will need careful stirring while it melts to make the mixture smooth.

Small quantities of butter or oil may safely be added to chocolate after it has been melted.

COCOA

Cocoa powder may be substituted for chocolate, if necessary, by using 3 tablespoons cocoa, 15 g (½ oz) butter and 1–2 tablespoons sugar for every 25 g (1 oz) chocolate required.

On the whole, I have specified cocoa in recipes only where it is preferable to chocolate; if you have none, use chocolate and adjust the butter and sugar accordingly.

WHICH CHOCOLATE AND WHICH COCOA?

Wherever I go, I buy some bars of chocolate to try out different countries' tastes, and to experiment with when I get home. The following, while by no means an exhaustive list of possibilities, are the brands that I have found the most successful in recipes.

Bittersweet Eating Chocolate
Baker's German's Sweet
Cadbury's Bournville Palin
Cadbury's Bournville Dark
Callebaut Dessert
Côte d'Or 'Extra Dry'
Côte d'Or Chocolat Extra Superieur
Hershey's Special Dark
Lindt Bittersweet
Lindt Excellence
Suchard Velma
Suchard Bittra

Cooking Chocolate

Baker's Unsweetened

Gibraltar

Hershey's Unsweetened

Menier Chocolat Patissier
   (either sweetened or unsweetened)

Peters Viking

Poulain Chocolat à Patisser
   (either sweetened or unsweetened)

Cocoa

Droste

Hershey

Poulain

van Houten

THE OTHER INGREDIENTS

BUTTER AND MARGARINE

Please use sweet butter where I have specified unsalted butter. I have only done so where salted butter used in the recipe would sadly coarsen the taste of the finished dish.

Where margarine will do just as well as butter, I have given the choice; where I have not done so, butter is definitely preferable.

CREAM, SOUR CREAM, AND YOGURT

I have indicated the best kind of cream to use in each recipe.

Cream in America is very different from cream in England, where it is much thicker and richer (i.e., has a higher butterfat content). For this reason, wherever the recipes call for cream, be it double, whipping, single, or a combination of these, it would be best to use heavy or whipping cream. I have found that heavy cream whips to a satisfactory consistency; the mixture will be lighter than in England, but this is no loss to the finished dish.

Sour cream and yogurt, on the other hand, seem to be thicker in America than in England, and where a recipe calls for whipped cream, the diet-conscious may sometimes like to use yogurt, or, best of all, a half-and-half mixture of yogurt and heavy cream.

Cream should never be whipped with an electric beater, though an electric mixer with a balloon whisk attachment may be used. The best way to whip cream (as egg whites) is by hand, in a large bowl, with a balloon whisk. Unfortunately, an egg is not just an egg—it comes in different sizes. Often this doesn't matter too much, but where stiffly whipped egg whites are called for, or where yolks are used to set a dish, add one extra if your eggs are very small.

LIQUEURS AND SPIRITS

Several recipes call for liqueurs or spirits, and in those cases I have often given a number of alternatives.

Where only one or two liqueurs or spirits are mentioned, these are the ones that I would most recommend, but in every case readers may like to substitute their own favourites, or experiment with different flavours at different times, or sometimes even omit them altogether. In the rare instances where I think a particular liqueur or spirit is really vital, I have made this clear in the recipe.

FLAVOURS

Some flavourings blend particularly well with chocolate, and these appear over and over again in the recipes.

Coffee and chocolate have a particular affinity, and a little of one invariably enhances the flavour of the other.

Cinnamon was much used by the Aztecs in conjunction with cocoa, and even now, Mexican chocolate often comes ready-flavoured with cinnamon. A little cinnamon deepens the flavour in a remarkable way. Although I have usually specified the quantities to use, it is a spice that loses its aroma quite quickly, so this should be borne in mind when cooking.

Vanilla, yet another native of South America, is usually already blended into chocolate at the manufacturing stage, but a little more often enhances the flavour of a dish.

As far as other flavours are concerned, I have unashamedly allowed my own tastes to rule, and have included only what I enjoy eating. This may have led to serious omissions in the eyes of some readers: for example, there is no recipe for marzipan, nor any that include coconut or dates, and very few that use ginger or raisins. Perhaps this will stimulate readers to use their imagination and experiment with their own favourite flavours.

QUANTITIES AND MEASUREMENTS

It is always difficult to say how many people a given dish will feed. Cakes, biscuits and confectionary speak for themselves, but, unless specified otherwise, the quantities given for desserts are roughly for four to six people, depending on greed.

The first measurements given in the recipes are British metric, followed by British imperial measurements in parentheses. These are the same as American measurements. The cup and spoon equivalents of these metric and imperial measurements are given in the List of Equivalents that follows.

INGREDIENTS, COOKING EQUIPMENT, AND TERMINOLOGY

A few of the ingredients called for may seem unfamiliar to American readers, as will some English names for cooking equipment, and other terminology. The American counterparts for all of these are given in the List of Equivalents that follows.

LIST OF EQUIVALENTS

Ingredients

bicarbonate of soda = baking soda

biscuits = cookies

bitter chocolate = bittersweet chocolate

candied peel = candied fruit rind

caster sugar = superfine sugar

cornflour = cornstarch

curd cheese = farmer's cheese

digestive biscuits = graham crackers
   (chocolate digestive biscuits = chocolate-covered graham crackers)

double cream = heavy or whipping cream

ginger nuts = ginger cookies

golden syrup = thick corn syrup, or honey (if using corn syrup, it should be boiled until it thickens a bit)

icing sugar = confectioners' sugar

plain chocolate = semisweet or bittersweet chocolate

plain flour = all-purpose flour

salad oil = vegetable oil

self-raising flour = all-purpose flour with baking powder added (5 teaspoons per pound, or 1¼ teaspoons per 4 ounces)

shortcrust pastry = piecrust pastry
single cream = heavy or whipping cream
soured cream = sour cream
top of the milk = light cream, or half and half
trifle sponges = lady fingers or sponge cake

Measurements

butter 25 g (1 oz) = 2 tablespoons
    125 g (4 oz) = ½ cup or 1 stick
flour 25 g (1 oz) = 4 tablespoons
    125 g (4 oz) = 1 cup
sugar 25 g (1 oz) = 2 tablespoons
icing (confectioners') sugar 25 g (1 oz) = 4 tablespoons
    125 g (4 oz) = 1 cup

Liquid measurements

75 ml (⅛ pint) = ¼ cup + 1 tablespoon
150 ml (¼ pint) = ⅔ cup
300 ml (½ pint) = 1¼ cups
600 ml (1 pint) = 2½ cups
vanilla sugar = sugar flavoured with vanilla
white bread flour = all-purpose flour

Cooking Equipment and Terminology

to bake blind = to bake empty, as a piecrust
baking sheet = cookie sheet
baking tin = square cake pan
baking tray = cookie sheet
butter paper = buttered wax paper
dessertspoon = a spoon that is of a size halfway between a
    teaspoon and a tablespoon
flan tin = round cake pan
greaseproof paper = kitchen parchment paper
piping bag = pastry bag
pudding basin = ceramic mixing bowl with high sides
rice paper = edible wafer paper used for baking on; comes
    in sheets or small rounds

sandwich tin = cake pan
sponge tin = cake pan
sugar thermometer = candy thermometer

RECIPES

'Are they all your own?' 'Did you make them all up?'
friends will ask from time to time. No, of course not. Who
would wish to invent a 'new' recipe for such classics as
brownies, *profiteroles* or *Schwarzwälder Kirschtorte*? But
there are always many variations on these themes, and it is
a cookery writer's task to give the method which he or she
has found the most reliably successful, set out—I hope—in
a way that is easy to follow.

From time to time, of course, there is the excitement of
'inventing' a new dish. Often one finds later that there is
nothing new under the sun, even in cooking, but just
occasionally a new combination, juxtaposition or even a
method is truly original—though if the dish is attractive, it
quickly goes into general circulation. But then, that is what
cooking is all about—it is essentially a craft designed for
shared pleasure.

And finally, one recipe that I give here, because it is
almost a basic ingredient for many dishes.

PRALINE

Praline is said to have been invented, like so many of the
happiest culinary innovations, as the result of an accident.
The story goes that a kitchen boy in the household of the
Duc de Plessis-Praslin dropped a bowl of almonds on the
floor. The chef, in his anger, burnt a panful of sugar and
then spilt it over the almonds. In rage and despair, he

served up the caramelized almonds as a dessert—and the duke was delighted.

Make this in a large quantity, as it keeps indefinitely in a screw-top jar.

500 G (1 LB) ALMONDS OR HAZELNUTS, OR A COMBINATION OF
    THE TWO
225 G (8 OZ) SUGAR
4 TABLESPOONS WATER

Blanch the almonds and roast or toast them till golden brown. Roast or toast hazelnuts till golden brown, then blow off the loose skins (out of doors or into the sink).

Melt the sugar with the water in a heavy saucepan over moderate heat and when it turns liquid, but before it begins to colour, add the nuts and stir until they are all well coated. As soon as the caramel has turned golden brown, remove it from the heat and pour out onto a wooden board or large, lightly oiled plate.

Leave to cool, then peel off and place in a plastic bag and crush with a rolling pin or grind in a mortar, blender or food processor.

In America, you can also buy pralines in candy stores and then crush them for use in the recipes.

EQUIPMENT

No special equipment is needed for any of these recipes, and even in the confectionery chapter I have confined myself to recipes that can be made in the average kitchen. However, an electric mixer, a blender, a food processor and a candy thermometer are all invaluable aids.

Americain auec
Sa Choco
latiere
et Son
Gobelet

Rameau de Lárbre
du Cacao

Cacao

Gousses de Vanille

From Dufour's *Treatise on Coffee, Tea and Chocolate*, 1685

CHAPTER
1

SAVOURY DISHES

These recipes may come as a shock to the modern reader, but they would not have surprised our ancestors.

Chocolate began as a spiced drink and an ingredient in savoury dishes, and continued to be used as such long after the Spanish had discovered how much nicer it tasted sweet. In Italy there were recipes for chocolate pasta, and there is a shop in Venice where to this day you can buy cocoa-flavoured tagliatelli.

These few recipes are worth trying – the small amount of chocolate (which should be unsweetened, but can be bitter if necessary) only deepens the flavour without dominating the dish.

Sixteenth-century engraving of Aztec women roasting and grinding cocoa

BRAISED PIGEON WITH CHOCOLATE

Surprisingly fresh and uncloying, this is especially good served on a bed of mashed root vegetables such as potatoes, celeriac or Jerusalem artichokes.

4 PIGEONS
2 CLOVES GARLIC
SALT AND FRESHLY GROUND BLACK PEPPER
40 G (1½ OZ) BUTTER
2 TABLESPOONS OIL
4 LARGE SPANISH ONIONS
150 ML (¼ PINT) WHITE WINE
300 ML (½ PINT) STOCK
15 G (½ OZ) UNSWEETENED CHOCOLATE
1 TABLESPOON FLOUR
SQUEEZE OF LEMON JUICE

Wipe the pigeons well inside and out and rub them with the cut surface of one of the garlic cloves, then rub them with salt and pepper.

Melt 25 g (1 oz) of the butter with the oil in a heavy flameproof casserole large enough to hold the pigeons sitting side by side, and quickly brown them all over. Set aside and keep warm.

Slice the onions and the remaining garlic finely and sweat gently in the casserole until they are soft and golden yellow.

Return the pigeons to the casserole. Add the wine and stock, bring to the boil, then cover and simmer for 40 minutes–1 hour, or until the pigeons are tender. (The best test is to move a leg – if it feels quite loose, the bird is done.)

Remove the pigeons from the casserole and keep hot.

Bring the stock to the boil, allow to boil fast for 2–3 minutes to reduce a little, then remove the casserole from the heat. Add the chocolate and stir until it has dissolved and is fully amalgamated.

Make a *beurre manié* by working the flour into the remaining butter and add to the stock. Stir over gentle heat until the sauce begins to thicken. Add the squeeze of lemon juice, taste for seasoning, return the pigeons to heat through, and serve.

Indian podding cocoa beans, 1867

CHOCOLATE DUCK

A very satisfying winter dish, best served with rice or a purée of root vegetables.

I ROASTING DUCK
2 ONIONS, FINELY SLICED
2 CARROTS, FINELY SLICED
I TABLESPOON OIL
4 TABLESPOONS WINE VINEGAR
150 ML ($\frac{1}{4}$ PINT) WHITE WINE OR CHICKEN STOCK
2 TABLESPOONS DRY SHERRY
BOUQUET GARNI — BAY LEAF, SPRIG OF PARSLEY AND
   THYME
25 G (I OZ) UNSWEETENED CHOCOLATE
SALT AND FRESHLY GROUND BLACK PEPPER
LEMON JUICE

Wipe the duck inside and out and prick it well all over with a sharp-pronged fork.

Heat the oil in a flameproof casserole and gently brown the vegetables, then lift them out of the casserole and set aside.

Raise the heat and brown the duck all over in the casserole. Lift it out and drain off all the fat.

Add the vinegar to the casserole and cook until almost evaporated. Pour in the wine or stock and the sherry, return the vegetables and the duck to the casserole, add the bouquet garni, cover and simmer for about 1$\frac{1}{2}$ hours, or until the juice from the duck, when pricked, runs out just clear.

Take the duck out of the casserole and joint it. Keep hot.

Skim off any excess fat from the casserole. Add the chocolate to the sauce and stir until melted. Add seasoning and a good squeeze of lemon juice to taste, return the pieces of duck and heat through.

Ekchuah, god of the cocoa planters

MOLE POBLANO DE GUAJOLOTE
Turkey in chilli and chocolate sauce

From *The Book of Latin American Cooking* by Elisabeth Lambert Ortiz published by Jill Norman Ltd (1981). Reprinted by kind permission of the author and publisher.

This is Mexico's most famous dish and though it is native to the state of Puebla, it is served all over the republic on truly festive occasions. It can be absolutely sensational for a party when served with tortillas, Mexican rice and beans, and *guacamole* (avocado sauce). I always put a small bowl of canned *serrano* or *jalapeno* chillies on the table for the bold souls who claim no dish is hot enough for them. Actually, *mole poblano* is not hot, though I have come across versions of it where a *chipolle* chilli or two had been added, introducing both heat and this chilli's very exotic flavour. For a more everyday dish, chicken or pork may be used instead of turkey.

There is a charming but apocryphal legend that a group of nuns at the convent of Santa Rosa in Puebla invented the dish in early colonial times to honour a visiting viceroy and archbishop. But, in fact, it had long been a royal dish of the Aztec court. It is on record that the Spanish *conquistador* Hernán Cortés was served a version of the dish at the court of the Aztec Emperor Montezuma. All the same I do think we owe the sisters a debt. They recorded the recipe, which might otherwise have been lost, and they substituted familiar ingredients for some of the more exotic herbs and spices used in the Emperor's day. I'd be prepared to swear that in the past

allspice (a native spice) was used instead of cloves and
cinnamon brought by Spain from the East, but since the
flavour is much the same, why fuss?

Since *mole*, which comes from the Nahuatl word *molli*,
means a sauce made from any of the chillies, hot, pungent,
or sweet, there are more *moles* in Mexico than one can count.
Out of the innumerable array, I have had to content myself
with just this one. However, it can be made with chicken
instead of turkey, either halving the amount of sauce for one
chicken or using two 1½–1¾ kilo (3–3½ lb) chickens, cut
into serving pieces. It is also delicious made with pork: use
1½ kilos (3 lb) lean, boneless pork cut into 4 cm (2 in) pieces
and simmer gently in water barely to cover for 1 hour. Add
the pork to the sauce and simmer, covered, until the pork is
tender, about 30 minutes. Left-over *mole* makes a splendid
filling for *tacos*.

Serves 10
A 4 KILO (8 LB) TURKEY, CUT INTO SERVING PIECES
1 MEDIUM ONION, CHOPPED
2 CLOVES GARLIC, CHOPPED
SALT
90 G (3 OZ) LARD

For the sauce
6 *ancho* CHILLIES
6 *mulato* CHILLIES
4 *pasilla* CHILLIES
2 MEDIUM ONIONS, CHOPPED
3 CLOVES GARLIC, CHOPPED
3 MEDIUM TOMATOES, PEELED, SEEDED, AND CHOPPED
2 TORTILLAS, OR 2 SLICES TOAST, CUT UP
120 G (4 OZ) BLANCHED ALMONDS
60 G (2 OZ) PEANUTS
90 G (3 OZ) RAISINS
4 TABLESPOONS SESAME SEEDS

½ TEASPOON GROUND CORIANDER SEED
½ TEASPOON GROUND ANISE
2 WHOLE CLOVES
A 1 CM (½ IN) PIECE OF STICK CINNAMON
120 G (4 OZ) LARD
45 G (1½ OZ) PLAIN CHOCOLATE
SALT AND FRESHLY GROUND PEPPER
1 TABLESPOON SUGAR (OPTIONAL)

Put the turkey pieces into a large heavy saucepan with the onion, garlic, and water to cover. Season with salt and bring to the boil; lower the heat and simmer, covered, for about an hour, or until the turkey is barely tender. Drain off and reserve the turkey stock. Lift out the turkey pieces and pat them dry with paper towels. Heat the lard in a large pan and sauté the turkey pieces until they are lightly browned on both sides. Set them aside.

To make the sauce: remove the stems and seeds from the *ancho, mulato,* and *pasilla* chillies. Tear them into pieces, put them in a bowl, and pour about 450 ml (¾ pint) hot water over them – barely to cover. Let them stand for 30 minutes, turning the pieces from time to time. In a blender or food processor, combine the chillies and the water in which they have soaked with the onions, garlic, tomatoes, and tortillas or toast, and blend the mixture until it forms a paste. Do this in two lots if necessary. Transfer the paste to a bowl.

Rinse out and dry the container of the blender or food processor and add the almonds, peanuts, raisins, 2 tablespoons of the sesame seeds, the coriander seed, the anise, the cloves and the cinnamon stick, broken up, and blend the mixture well. Mix thoroughly with the chilli paste. Measure the lard left in the pan from sautéing the turkey and add enough to bring the quantity up to 60 g (2 oz). Add the chilli paste and sauté over moderate heat, stirring, for 5 minutes. Transfer the mixture to the saucepan in which the turkey was cooked. Stir in 450 ml (¾ pint) of the reserved turkey stock and the chocolate. Season to taste with salt and pepper. Cook the mixture over low heat, stirring until the chocolate is melted and adding more turkey stock if necessary to make the sauce the consistency of double cream. Stir in the sugar, if liked. Add the turkey pieces and simmer, covered, for 30 minutes. Arrange the turkey and sauce in a serving dish.

In a small pan, toast the remaining sesame seeds and sprinkle them over the turkey. Serve with tortillas, *arroz blanco* [white rice], *frijoles* [beans], and *guacamole* [avocado sauce].

*　　*　　*　　*　　*　　*　　*　　*　　*

There was a young gourmet of Crediton
Who took pâté de foie gras and spread it on
A chocolate biscuit.
He murmured 'I'll risk it.'
His tomb bears the date that he said it on.

Anon

*　　*　　*　　*　　*　　*　　*　　*　　*

THE ROYAL RECIPE
FOR HARE

The recipe for this excellent dish is reprinted, by kind permission of the author and publisher, from Elisabeth Ayrton's *The Cookery of England*, published by André Deutsch (1974).

This recipe is best of all for wild boar, but it is also excellent with hare or venison. It comes from the collection of Norman Douglas. The original recipe has 60 g (2 oz) pine nuts rather than almonds, but either is very good.

1 SADDLE OF HARE
60 G (2 OZ) BUTTER

THE MEAT IS MARINATED IN THE FOLLOWING MARINADE
    FOR ABOUT 12 HOURS:
300 ML ($\frac{1}{2}$ PINT) DRY WHITE WINE
2 CARROTS, FINELY SLICED
2 MEDIUM ONIONS, FINELY SLICED
1 CLOVE GARLIC
1 STICK CELERY, SLICED
1 BAY LEAF
3 CLOVES
SPRIGS OF PARSLEY AND THYME

Turn the saddle of hare in the marinade several times and spoon the vegetables and liquids over it.

Melt the butter in a large saucepan or Dutch oven. Remove the hare and the vegetables from the marinade and brown all slightly in the butter. When brown, set on a low heat and gradually spoon all the marinade liquor over the hare and vegetables, a little every few minutes, covering it in between. Very slowly simmer, covered, for 1–1$\frac{1}{4}$ hours.

Meanwhile, prepare the sauce.

30 G (1 OZ) CASTER SUGAR
1 TABLESPOON WINE VINEGAR
60 G (2 OZ) BLANCHED AND HALVED ALMONDS
30 G (1 OZ) STONED RAISINS AND
30 G (1 OZ) CURRANTS, SOAKED TOGETHER IN A LITTLE
    WATER
60 G (2 OZ) BITTER CHOCOLATE, FINELY GRATED

Put the sugar into a saucepan with a teaspoonful of water and caramelize over heat. Add a tablespoon of wine vinegar and bring to the boil. Leave to cool.

When the hare is done, remove from the pan and keep hot. Strain into the sugar/vinegar sauce half of the liquid in which the hare was cooking. Add the blanched and halved almonds, raisins, currants and bitter chocolate. Stir for 2 minutes. This sauce is wonderful with the strong hare or venison meat, as the chocolate brings out the flavour without being really discernible. It can be served separately and the hare carved at table, or the hare may be carved in slices in the kitchen and the sauce poured over. Be careful to keep it very hot.

Plain rice or boiled potatoes are best with this dish and red wine, rough cider, or beer should be drunk with it. It calls for something more definite than water.

'*Le marchand de coco*', from *Cris de Paris*, 1774

HOW THE GOOD NEWS WAS BROUGHT FROM THE NEW WORLD TO SPAIN

Everyone knows that chocolate came from the New World. Today we think of chocolate as a restorative drink, as a delicious form of confectionery and as an essential ingredient for some of the richest desserts of western cuisines. In the days of the Aztecs and Mayans, however, the cacao bean was used as the basis for a drink which had an important ceremonial function.

Chocolate was drunk and cacao beans were offered to deities at many rituals, including those for the naming of infants and the puberty rites of young children, when a marriage was arranged or a funeral took place. Chocolate was served to valiant fighters, but withheld from the cowardly: 'He will not receive tobacco. He will not drink chocolate; he will not eat fine foods.'

Among the Mayans, the cacao planters, like the members of every other trade, had their own god, Ekchuah, whose festival – held in the month of Muan – seems to have been jollier than most. At least Ekchuah extorted no human sacrifice, only that of a dog with a cocoa-coloured spot.

The planting of cacao trees was also a ritual occasion. According to the nineteenth-century historian H. H. Bancroft, 'the finest grains of seed were exposed to the moonlight during four nights, and ... the tillers of the soil

A map of the five world regions from the Codex Féjerváry-Mayer, Mixtec, mid fourteenth century; the central top panel represents a cocoa tree

must sleep apart from their wives and concubines for several days, in order that on the night before planting they might indulge their passions to the fullest extent; certain persons were even said to have been appointed to perform the sexual act at the very moment when the first seeds were deposited in the ground.'

The cacao bean was the nearest approach to a standard currency in Central America. Tributes were paid from one state to another and purchases made in cacao beans. While a pumpkin, for instance, might cost 4 cacao nibs and a rabbit 10, a 'tolerably good' slave would cost one hundred. You

Indians worshipping a column with offerings of cocoa and other fruit, de Bry, 1591

could also buy a woman's favours with chocolate ... To quote Bancroft again, 'Public prostitution was tolerated if not encouraged by all the Mayan nations. In every Nicaraguan town, there were establishments kept by public women, who sold their favours for 10 cacao nibs.'

Since cacao nibs were currency ('Blessed money, which exempts its possessors from avarice, since it cannot be long hoarded nor hidden underground,' wrote the historian, Peter Martyr), they came to be used as symbols for numbers, and it may well be that the handling of nibs in their hundreds and thousands contributed to the Mayans' complex grasp of arithmetic.

It was not Columbus's fault that he failed to be the one to introduce chocolate to the old world. He certainly must have come across the drink when he landed, probably in what is now Nicaragua, in 1502, for he brought cocoa beans home with him and presented them to King Ferdinand. Unfortunately neither the King nor anyone else at court showed any interest.

So the honour went to Cortés. When he and his band of Spanish soldiers landed on the shores of Mexico seventeen years later, in 1519, they were surprised and suspicious to be immediately welcomed by emissaries from the magnificent ruler Montezuma. The reason lay in Aztec mythology, where the feathered serpent god Quetzacoatl, who had taught his people how to read the stars and given them a calendar, had also brought the seeds of the cacao tree from the Garden of Life. Like Prometheus, he paid dearly for his generosity to man, being tricked by a rival god into drinking a potion that robbed him of his godly powers. He buried his wealth, changed his royal cacao trees into thorny mesquite shrubs and went into exile, promising his people that he

Example of Aztec numbering denoting 20 × 1600. A flag indicated 20, while baskets denoted 1600, being the number of cocoa nibs contained in each basket

would return one day from the east. So when Cortés landed on the east coast of Mexico, he was given a respectful welcome – for who could be sure the stranger was not the reincarnated god?

At the resplendent court of Montezuma, the Spaniards were introduced to the royal drink xocoatl. One of Cortés' soldiers, the twenty-four-year-old Bernal Díaz del Castillo, kept a detailed account of the campaign and published it in his old age, prefacing it with 'Oh, what a troublesome thing it is to go and discover new lands and the risks we took it is hardly possible to exaggerate ...'

He describes how Montezuma took his chocolate:

Montezuma's food was served on Cholula ware, some red and some black. While he was dining, the guards in the adjoining rooms did not dare to speak or make a noise above a whisper ... Sometimes they brought him in cups of pure gold, a drink made from the cocoa-plant, which they said he took before visiting his wives ... I saw them bring in a good fifty large jugs of this chocolate, all frothed up, of which he would drink a little. They always served it with great reverence. Sometimes some little hump-backed dwarfs would be present at his meals, whose bodies seemed almost to be broken in the middle. These were his jesters. There were other Indians who told him jokes and must have been his clowns, and others who sang and danced, for Montezuma was very fond of music and entertainment and would reward his entertainers with the leavings of the food and chocolate ...

As soon as the great Montezuma had dined, all the guards and many more of his household servants ate in their turn. I think more than a thousand plates of food must have been brought in for them, and more than two thousand jugs of chocolate frothed up in the Mexican style, and infinite quantities of fruit, so that with his women and serving maids and bread-makers and chocolate-makers his expenses must have been considerable.

The Spaniards repaid Montezuma's hospitality by cruelly slaughtering him and conquering his city. In 1521 the *conquistadors* left Mexico, returning to Spain by way of Africa. There they planted some cocoa trees from Mexican seeds and so set the foundation for the Spanish monopoly in the cocoa trade which was to last for at least a hundred years.

Unlike Columbus, Cortés valued not only the gold and silver that his conquests brought, but also the strange and bitter drink he had drunk at Montezuma's court. He recognized its energy-giving properties: '*Una taza de este preciosa brebaje permete de andar un dia entero sin tomar alimento*' ('one cup of this precious drink allows a man to walk a whole day without taking nourishment').

Back home he introduced the drink to the Spanish court. To the bitter and highly spiced Mexican recipe, the Spanish added vanilla and sugar, both also recently imported from the New World, and the drink quickly became the vogue at court and in high society.

Cacaoyer.

CHAPTER
2

HOT DESSERTS

Man grinding cocoa beans, 1687

MAKING HOT SOUFFLÉS

A hot soufflé, with its lightly crusted top and creamy inside, miraculously standing a few inches proud of the dish, is an unfailingly impressive dessert. Once you have mastered the basic technique, however, a soufflé is simple to make and, although it must be brought to table as soon as it comes out of the oven, most of the preparations can be done well in advance, leaving only the whisked egg whites to be folded in at the last moment before baking. If the basic preparation has been done well ahead, the mixture will need to be warmed slightly before folding in the whites.

A soufflé can be baked in any deep round ovenproof dish, but it looks best when made in a proper soufflé dish: a round white, golden or brown pottery or porcelain dish with straight sides, narrowly ridged on the outside to give a pleated effect.

The dish must be buttered generously inside, and for a sweet soufflé it should be thoroughly sprinkled with caster sugar or finely ground nuts before pouring in the mixture.

The finished soufflé will look particularly effective if you use a dish that will just hold the basic mixture and tie a collar round it to allow the soufflé to rise. Use a piece of greaseproof paper or foil long enough to go round the dish with a generous overlap, and wide enough to fold down once or twice to make a 10 cm (4 in) wide strip. Stroke the folded strip firmly on the table to make it smooth and flexible, then butter generously and sprinkle with sugar. Fix it securely round the dish, buttered side in, tying it just under the top of the dish, where there is usually a ridge or rim to keep it firm. Remove the foil or paper collar just before serving.

Never use a dish bigger than the one indicated in the recipe. If you prefer, you can use two smaller dishes, or six to eight ramekins, but you will have to adjust the cooking time accordingly. (The smaller the dish, the shorter the cooking time.)

A soufflé should always be brought straight from the oven to the table, and placed on a large plate as it may spill over when first broken into. To make it look particularly elegant, enfold the base of the dish in a starched white napkin.

Indians harvesting and grinding cocoa

SIMPLE CHOCOLATE SOUFFLÉ

25 G (1 OZ) CORNFLOUR
250 ML (SCANT ½ PINT) MILK
100 G (3½ OZ) PLAIN OR BITTER CHOCOLATE
2 TEASPOONS INSTANT COFFEE POWDER (OPTIONAL)
50 G (2 OZ) SUGAR
3 EGG YOLKS
5 EGG WHITES
PINCH OF SALT
1 TABLESPOON CASTER SUGAR
1 TABLESPOON ICING SUGAR, SIFTED

Prepare a 1-litre (2-pint) soufflé dish as described on page 45 and set the oven at gas mark 5 (190°C) 375°F.

Mix the cornflour to a smooth thin paste with a little of the milk. Put remaining milk into a heavy saucepan, add the chocolate, the coffee dissolved in a few drops of boiling water, and the sugar, and stir over a gentle heat until the chocolate has completely melted and the sugar has dissolved.

Pour in the cornflour paste in a thin stream, stirring constantly, then bring the mixture to the boil and boil for 1 minute, still stirring continuously. Remove from the heat.

Separate the eggs and beat in the yolks one by one. Leave to cool a little.

The soufflé can be prepared ahead of time up to this point, but should, if necessary, be warmed a little before the next stage.

Whisk the whites with the pinch of salt until they begin to stand in soft peaks, then gradually beat in the caster sugar and continue to beat until they stand in stiff peaks but are not dry.

Now stir one third of the whites into the chocolate mixture until well blended, then fold the mixture gently but thoroughly into the remaining whites.

Pour immediately into the prepared soufflé dish and cook in the centre of the oven for 40 minutes.

Pull the soufflé gently to the front of the oven, sprinkle with a little of the sifted icing sugar and close the oven door again. After a few minutes, the icing sugar should have melted. Sprinkle with a little more, and repeat another two or three times until all the icing sugar has been used. This will give the soufflé an attractive glaze.

Serve immediately.

ECONOMICAL CHOCOLATE
SOUFFLÉ

A good family dessert for a cold day. To make it slightly more luxurious, you can substitute 50 g (2 oz) ground almonds for half the breadcrumbs.

50 G (2 OZ) PLAIN OR BITTER CHOCOLATE
250 ML (SCANT ½ PINT) MILK
50 G (2 OZ) SOFT WHITE BREADCRUMBS
25 G (I OZ) BUTTER
100 G (3½ OZ) SUGAR
3 EGGS
PINCH OF SALT

Prepare a ½-litre (1-pint) soufflé dish as described on page 45 and set the oven at gas mark 5 (190°C) 375°F.

Break the chocolate into the milk and bring it gently to the boil, stirring until the chocolate has melted.

Remove from the heat and add the breadcrumbs, the butter and sugar and stir until smooth.

Separate the eggs and add the yolks one by one, stirring until they are well blended.

The soufflé can be prepared ahead of time up to this point, but should, if necessary, be slightly warmed before adding the whisked egg whites.

Whisk the whites with the pinch of salt until they stand in stiff peaks, then fold in the chocolate mixture and pour into the prepared soufflé dish. Bake for 45–50 minutes, until the top is well risen and firm.

Serve immediately.

RICH CHOCOLATE
LIQUEUR SOUFFLÉ

This is excellent made with Tia Maria, Grand Marnier or orange curaçao or you can use a chocolate peppermint liqueur.

300 ML (½ PINT) MILK
I TABLESPOON INSTANT COFFEE POWDER
25 G (I OZ) PLAIN OR BITTER CHOCOLATE
2 TABLESPOONS SUGAR
50 G (2 OZ) UNSALTED BUTTER
2 TABLESPOONS FLOUR
4 EGG YOLKS
2 TABLESPOONS BRANDY
2 TABLESPOONS LIQUEUR (SEE ABOVE)
½ TEASPOON VANILLA ESSENCE
5 EGG WHITES
I DESSERTSPOON CASTER SUGAR
PINCH OF SALT

Prepare a 1-litre (2-pint) soufflé dish as described on page 45, and set the oven at gas mark 6 (200°C) 400°F.

Scald the milk, then remove it from the heat and add the coffee, chocolate and sugar and stir until smooth.

Melt the butter in a heavy saucepan, add the flour and stir till smooth. Cook over a gentle heat for 2 minutes, stirring constantly. Do not allow it to colour.

Remove from the heat, and gradually add the chocolate milk, stirring constantly to keep the mixture smooth.

Separate the eggs and stir in the yolks one by one. Then add the brandy, liqueur and vanilla.

The soufflé can be prepared ahead of time up to this point, but should, if necessary, be warmed a little before folding in the whisked egg whites.

Whisk the 5 whites with the pinch of salt until they begin to stand in soft peaks, then gradually beat in the caster sugar. Continue to beat until they stand in stiff peaks but are not dry.

Gently stir one third of the whites into the chocolate mixture until well blended, then fold in the remaining whites lightly but thoroughly.

Pour into the prepared soufflé dish and cook for 40 minutes in the centre of the oven.

Serve immediately.

CHOCOLATE ALMOND SOUFFLÉ

Very rich, but amazingly light.

125 G (4 OZ) PLAIN OR BITTER CHOCOLATE
2 TABLESPOONS MILK
4 EGGS
100 G (3½ OZ) CASTER SUGAR
50 G (2 OZ) GROUND ALMONDS
1 TABLESPOON FLOUR
150 ML (¼ PINT) DOUBLE CREAM

Prepare a ½-litre (1-pint) soufflé dish as described on page 45 and set the oven at gas mark 6 (200°C) 400°F.

Break the chocolate into the milk and heat it gently, stirring until the chocolate has melted and the mixture is smooth. Leave to cool.

Separate the eggs and whisk the yolks with the sugar until pale and fluffy. Sift the ground almonds with the flour and beat into the yolks, then beat in the melted chocolate and the cream.

The soufflé can be prepared ahead of time up to this point, but should, if necessary, be warmed a little before folding in the whisked egg whites.

Whisk the egg whites till they stand in soft peaks and fold them into the mixture. Pour into the prepared soufflé dish and cook in the centre of the oven for about 40 minutes. The top should be dry and almost crisp, the edges of the soufflé lightly set and the centre creamily runny.

Serve immediately.

CHOCOLATE FRUIT RING

Served hot or warm, this is remarkably light for such a rich dessert, and any left-overs are just as good served slightly warmed the following day. It is particularly good made with crystallized orange slices and pecan nuts, but mixed crystallized fruit and any other nuts you prefer will also be excellent. Serve alone or with a little whipped cream or home-made custard.

200 G (7 OZ) PLAIN OR BITTER CHOCOLATE
175 G (6 OZ) CRYSTALLIZED FRUIT (SEE ABOVE)
175 G (6 OZ) NUTS (SEE ABOVE)
6 EGGS
150 G (5 OZ) ICING SUGAR
2 TEASPOONS INSTANT COFFEE POWDER

Set the oven to gas mark 5 (190°C) 375°F.
    Butter and flour a 22 cm (9 in) ring mould or gugelhopf tin.
    Melt the chocolate (see page 13) and leave to cool.
    Chop the fruit and nuts fairly finely.
    Separate the eggs and whisk the yolks with the icing sugar (this gives more body than caster sugar) until they form a really thick light sponge.
    Dissolve the instant coffee in the minimum of hot water and add to the yolks.
    When the chocolate has cooled, blend it into the yolks together with the chopped fruit and nuts.
    Whip the whites until they form soft peaks and fold very lightly but evenly into the mixture.

Pour into the prepared tin and bake in the centre of the oven for 40–45 minutes. Leave to cool for a few minutes, then turn carefully out of the mould.

Dust with a little more icing sugar and serve hot or warm.

STEAMED CHOCOLATE SPONGE PUDDING

Very light, and not at all like the dreaded puddings of school memory. Serve with lightly whipped cream or with a home-made custard laced, if you like, with a little brandy.

125 G (4 OZ) BUTTER
125 G (4 OZ) CASTER SUGAR
175 G (6 OZ) FLOUR
1 TEASPOON BAKING POWDER
25 G (1 OZ) COCOA POWDER
PINCH OF SALT
2 LARGE EGGS
2 TABLESPOONS MILK

Cream the butter and sugar until very light and fluffy.

Sift the flour, baking powder, cocoa and salt together. Beat the eggs together lightly with the milk and add alternately with the sifted flour mixture to the creamed butter and sugar and beat in well.

Pour into a buttered 1-litre (2-pint) pudding basin, lay a piece of buttered greaseproof paper over the top and then cover with a piece of foil, pleated to allow for the pudding to rise. Tie string tightly round the neck of the basin and set it on an upturned saucer in a pan of simmering water. There should not be more than 5 cm (2 in) of water, but check that the pan does not boil dry.

Steam the pudding for 1½–2 hours. Turn out on to a heated dish before serving.

CHOCOLATE BAKED ALASKA

A spectacular dessert, and one that is really very easy to make. If you do not have time to make your own ice cream, use a good quality bought one.

You can prepare this dessert three or four days ahead, and keep in the freezer (any longer and the meringue will begin to collapse).

6 TRIFLE SPONGES
2 TABLESPOONS VERY STRONG BLACK COFFEE
4 TABLESPOONS BRANDY
600 ML (1 PINT) ECONOMICAL OR RICH CHOCOLATE ICE
    CREAM (SEE PAGES 123–4)
3 EGG WHITES
75 G (3 OZ) CASTER SUGAR
1 TABLESPOON GRANULATED SUGAR

Split the sponge cakes and line a shallow ovenproof dish with them, making sure that the bottom and sides of the dish are completely covered.

Blend the coffee with 2 tablespoons of the brandy and dribble over the sponge cakes.

Spoon on the ice cream and smooth it off, so that it makes an even mound on top of the sponge base, but leaves a generous 2 cm (1 in) margin round the edge of the dish. Place in the freezer while you make the meringue.

Whip the egg whites until they stand in soft peaks, then slowly whip in the caster sugar until you have a stiff, glossy meringue mixture. Smooth this over the top and sides of the ice cream and sponge cake so that everything is sealed by a layer of meringue at least 2.5 cm (1 in) thick. Sprinkle with the granulated sugar and replace in the freezer until needed.

Have the oven ready at gas mark 7 (220°C) 425°F.

Place the Alaska straight from the freezer into the oven and bake for 15 minutes, or until the meringue is just set and lightly browned.

Warm the remaining brandy.

As soon as the Alaska is ready, pour on the brandy, set alight and bring flaming to the table.

NOTE: You can use a liqueur (try Grand Marnier, Tia Maria or crème de menthe) instead of the brandy for soaking the sponge cakes: you can also blend a little of it into the ice cream. For flaming, however, it is best to use brandy.

For an even more extravagant dessert, sprinkle the ice cream thickly with coarsely crushed praline (see page 20) before coating with the meringue.

CHOCOLATE PANCAKES 1

Deceptively light and delicate, but chiefly for adults, as the alcohol is an important ingredient.

The amount of filling you use is very much a matter of personal taste: 150 ml ($\frac{1}{4}$ pint) of cream is on the mean side, 300 ml ($\frac{1}{2}$ pint) more than generous.

125 G (4 OZ) FLOUR
I HEAPED TABLESPOON ICING SUGAR
I TABLESPOON COCOA POWDER
2 EGGS
BARE 150 ML ($\frac{1}{4}$ PINT) MILK
BARE 150 ML ($\frac{1}{4}$ PINT) WATER
I TABLESPOON BRANDY
50 G (2 OZ) BUTTER (MELTED)
BUTTER FOR FRYING

For the filling
150–300 ML ($\frac{1}{4}$–$\frac{1}{2}$ PINT) WHIPPING CREAM (SEE ABOVE)
2–4 TABLESPOONS CRÈME DE CACAO
  or I–2 TABLESPOONS ICING SUGAR
25–50 G (I–2 OZ) CHOCOLATE CHIPS (OPTIONAL)

For serving
ICING SUGAR

Sift the flour, icing sugar and cocoa into a bowl, make a well in the centre and break in the eggs. Work the dry ingredients into the eggs and gradually add the milk and water until you have a smooth, light batter. Beat in the brandy and the melted butter. It is best to let the batter rest in a cool place or refrigerator for about an hour.

Meanwhile prepare the filling by whipping the cream. When it begins to thicken, whip in the crème de cacao or icing sugar, and when it is quite stiff, fold in the chocolate chips. Chill until ready to use.

These pancakes are rather fragile, so use a small frying pan, 15 cm (6 in) in diameter, or make small pancakes in the centre of a large pan.

Heat the pan, then add a knob of butter. When it is foaming, pour in enough batter to make a 15 cm (6 in) circle. Be careful not to pour in too much as the batter should be very thin. As soon as the mixture has set, turn over and fry quickly on the other side. When cooked, set aside to keep warm and repeat with remaining batter.

Just before serving, put a dollop of the cream filling on each pancake and roll up. Dredge lightly with icing sugar.

Chocolate advertisement, c. 1820

CHOCOLATE PANCAKES 2

You can make these as simple or as sophisticated as you like, to suit your public.

For the filling
100 G (3 OZ) CHOCOLATE
100 G (3 OZ) UNSALTED BUTTER
25 G (I OZ) ICING SUGAR OR A LITTLE MORE,
   ACCORDING TO TASTE
I TABLESPOON RUM OR BRANDY (OPTIONAL)
50 G (2 OZ) FINELY GROUND HAZELNUTS OR PRALINE,
   SEE PAGE 20 (OPTIONAL)

For the pancakes
125 G (4 OZ) FLOUR
PINCH OF SALT
I TABLESPOON ICING SUGAR
2 EGGS
300 ML (½ PINT) MILK
I TABLESPOON BRANDY OR WATER
25 G (I OZ) BUTTER, MELTED
BUTTER FOR FRYING
ICING SUGAR

Make the filling first. Melt the chocolate (see page 13) and leave to cool a little.

Beat the butter with the sugar until light and fluffy, then beat in the chocolate, the rum or brandy and the nuts or praline. Taste for sweetness and leave in the refrigerator to harden.

To make the pancakes: sift the flour, salt and icing sugar

into a bowl. Make a well in the centre and break in the eggs.
Work the flour into the eggs and gradually add the milk until
you have a smooth, light batter. Beat in the brandy or water
and the melted butter. The batter should have the consistency
of single cream. Let the batter rest awhile if possible.

Heat a heavy frying or pancake pan, about 20 cm (8 in)
diameter, add a knob of butter and as soon as it begins to
foam, pour in a small ladleful of the batter. Turn the pan to
cover the bottom completely, then pour back any excess
batter as the pancakes should be as thin as possible. Cook the
pancake on both sides, and set aside to keep warm. Repeat
with remaining batter.

When ready to serve, place some chocolate filling down
the centre of each pancake, roll it up and place on a heated
serving dish. Reheat briefly under the grill if necessary.

Dredge with icing sugar before serving.

Fig. V.

CHOCOLATE PROFITEROLES

These airy puffs, filled with a delicately flavoured whipped cream and lightly coated with bitter chocolate sauce, must be the well-nigh perfect dessert – light but rich, sweet but not cloying.

For the choux pastry
300 ML (½ PINT) WATER
100 G (3½ OZ) UNSALTED BUTTER
PINCH OF SALT
1 TEASPOON SUGAR
125 G (4½ OZ) FLOUR
4 EGGS

For the filling
300 ML (½ PINT) DOUBLE OR WHIPPING CREAM
VANILLA ESSENCE OR BRANDY
1 TEASPOON ICING SUGAR

For the sauce
150 ML (¼ PINT) WATER
1 TABLESPOON COCOA POWDER
200 G (7 OZ) PLAIN OR BITTER CHOCOLATE
15 G (½ OZ) BUTTER

To make the puffs: set the oven at gas mark 7 (220°C) 425°F.

Put the water into a large saucepan, add the butter roughly cut into pieces, the salt and the sugar and bring slowly to the boil, stirring until the butter has melted.

Sift the flour.

As soon as the water has come to the boil, take the saucepan off the heat and tip in all the flour. Beat with a wooden spoon until smooth, return to a moderate heat and continue to beat until the mixture forms a single, smooth, thick mass and leaves the sides of the pan clean. Remove the pan from the heat again and beat in the eggs one by one, adding each only when the previous one has been completely amalgamated.

Fill the mixture into a piping bag with a thick nozzle and pipe small mounds on to a greased baking sheet; or drop small mounds on to the baking sheet with a teaspoon, making them as smooth as possible.

Bake at the top of the oven for 20–25 minutes, until they are well risen and pale brown. Remove the puffs and turn the oven off. Make an incision with the tip of a sharp knife in the side of each puff to let out the steam, place it on its side on the baking sheet and return to the oven for 10 minutes or so to dry out, leaving the oven door open. Then leave to cool on a wire rack.

When the puffs are quite cold – and not too long before you are ready to serve the profiteroles – whip the cream with the vanilla or brandy and sugar. Fill each puff with the cream, using either a teaspoon or a piping bag and nozzle, and pile them on a serving dish.

To make the sauce: bring the water and cocoa to the boil, stirring until it is smooth, then boil for 1 minute. Remove the pan from the heat, break in the chocolate and stir until the chocolate has dissolved. Add the butter, cut into small pieces, to give the sauce a gloss, and stir until smooth.

Pour the hot sauce over the profiteroles and serve.

NOTE: The profiteroles can also be quickly filled with vanilla ice cream, which gives the added pleasure of contrasting temperatures.

CHOCOLATE STRUDEL

A great Viennese speciality, the *Strudel* can have many different fillings, not only apples. The making of strudel pastry is an art in itself: it needs to be rolled and pulled and eased till it is so thin you can read a newspaper through it, and all this without a single hole or tear. Luckily, it is possible to buy strudel pastry, already rolled and cut into paper-thin sheets, in delicatessen stores, or you can use '*filo* pastry', bought from Greek stores, which is the same thing.

To make a chocolate *Strudel* you can use a filling made of eggs and sugar whipped till light and foamy and mixed with grated chocolate, but I find this a little too sweet, and prefer the sweet-and-sour combination given here.

225 G (8 OZ) CURD CHEESE
50 G (2 OZ) SUGAR
1 EGG YOLK
6 STRUDEL PASTRY LEAVES
25 G (1 OZ) BUTTER
50 G (2 OZ) PLAIN OR BITTER CHOCOLATE OR CHOCOLATE
   CHIPS
50 G (2 OZ) BLANCHED ALMONDS
ICING SUGAR, FOR SPRINKLING

Set the oven at gas mark 6 (200°C) 400°F.

Put the curd cheese, sugar and egg yolk into a bowl and whisk until light and fluffy.

Spread a clean tea-towel on your work surface, and lay the first of the pastry leaves out quite flat on top.

Melt the butter without allowing it to become hot and brush some lightly over the pastry leaf.

Add the next leaf and repeat until all the pastry leaves are lying on top of each other, each one lightly brushed with butter.

Spread the cheese mixture evenly on top, taking care not to tear the pastry – it is best to dot the pastry with dollops of the mixture and then spread it gently.

Chop the chocolate up quite small, together with the almonds (if you are using chocolate chips there is no need to chop them further) and sprinkle evenly over the cheese. Now pick up the two corners of the tea-towel that are farthest away from you and allow the strudel to fall over and roll up towards you in a tight roll. When it reaches the end of the tea-towel, let it roll on to a buttered baking sheet.

Brush the top with a little more butter and place just above the centre of the oven. Bake for $\frac{1}{2}$ hour, brushing the top with melted butter once or twice during the baking time.

When the *Strudel* is ready, remove it from the oven, brush with remaining butter and sprinkle the top thickly with sifted icing sugar.

Serve hot or warm.

NOTE: If you have bought a packet of strudel pastry leaves and are not using them all at once, wrap in airtight wrapping and store in the freezer. They will keep there for many months, whereas they will only keep in the refrigerator for one or two weeks.

From Dufour's *Treatise on Coffee, Tea and Chocolate*, 1685

THE SPANISH MONOPOLY
AND
AN ECCLESIASTICAL
CONTROVERSY

Spain hugged the discovery of chocolate to itself for nearly a hundred years, although travellers in South America encountered the strange drink. Giralamo Benzoni, who set out from his native Milan in 1541 at the age of twenty-two, determined to go to 'those countries of the Indians, recently found, called by everybody the New World', described the drink as 'more suited for pigs than for men'. Later he changed his mind:

> I am upwards of a year in that country without ever being induced to taste this beverage; and when I passed through a tribe, if an Indian wished occasionally to give me some, he was very much surprised to see me refuse it, and went away laughing. But subsequently, wine failing, and unwilling to drink nothing but water, I did as others did. The flavour is somewhat bitter, but it satisfies and refreshes the body without intoxicating: the Indians esteem it above everything, wherever they are accustomed to it.

A hundred years later, when Thomas Gage, a young Dominican friar from England, was first offered cocoa during his travels to Spanish America in 1648, he called it a 'spicy, scummy drink' – not surprisingly when you read his description of how it was made:

> The *Cacao*, and the other ingredients must be beaten in a mortar

of stone, or (as the *Indians* use) ground upon a broad stone, which they call *Metate*, and is only made for that use. But first the ingredients are all to be dried, except the *Achiotte* (a red colouring agent), with care that they may be beaten to powder, keeping them still in stirring, that they be not burnt or become black; for if they be over-dried, they will be bitter and lose their Virtue. The Cinnamon and the long red Pepper are to be first beaten with the Anniseed, and then the *Cacao*, which must be beaten by little and little, till it be all powdred; and in the beating it must be turn'd round, that it may mix the better. Every one of these ingredients must be beaten by itself, and then all be put into the Vessel, where the *Cacao* is, which you must stir together with a Spoon, and then take out that Paste, and put it into the mortar, under which there must be a little Fire, after the confection is made, but if more Fire be put under than will only warm it, the unctuous part will dry away. The *Achiotte* also must be put in in the beating, that it may the better take the colour. When it is well beaten and incorporated (which will be known by the shortness of it) then with a Spoon is taken up some of the paste, which will be almost liquid, and made into Tablets, or else without a Spoon put into Boxes, and when it is cold it will be hard . . .

The manner of drinking it, is divers; the one (being the way most us'd in Mexico) is to take it hot with *Atolle* (a cornmeal gruel drink), dissolving a Tablet in hot Water, and then stirring and beating it in the Cup where it is to be drunk, with a *Molinet* (a wooden stick carved especially for mixing chocolate), and when it is well stirr'd to a scum or froth, then to fill the cup with hot *Atolle*, and so drink it sup by sup.

Since chocolate had become so popular in Spain, it came under papal scrutiny. In 1569, Pope Pius V was served a cup and found it so disgusting that he was sure no one would make a habit of drinking it, and there was no need therefore to ban it during Lent. But this did not satisfy ecclesiastic minds. Many learned treatises were written to determine

QVESTION MORAL
Si el Chocolate quebranta el
ayuno Eclesiastico.
Tratase de otras bebidas i confecciones,
que se vsan en varias Provincias
A D. Garcia de Avellaneda y Haro Conde
de Castrillo de la Camara de su Mag.
Comendador de la Obreria de los
Consejos de Estado y Guerra
Castilla, y Camara, y Governador
del Real de las Indias.
Por el Lic. Antonio de Leon Pinelo,
Relator del mismo Consejo.

Famam abstinen-
tiæ in delicijs que-
rimus. S. Hiero.

Non est hoc suscipe-
re abstinentiam sed
imitari Luxuriam.
S. August.

I. de Courbes F

Madrid. Por la Viuda de Iuan Gonçalez. Año. 1636.

whether chocolate was a drink or a food – and whether it was permissible to drink it on the church's fast days. Cardinal Brancaccio declared in 1662 that *'Liquidum non frangit jejunum'* ('the drinking of liquids does not break the fast'), but the controversy continued to rage on well into the eighteenth century.

In the Spanish provinces of the New World, as well as in Spain itself, the drinking of chocolate had become fashionable in high society. In Spanish America the nuns had discovered that the drink became more palatable when drunk warm or hot, and different convents vied with each other for the honour of having perfected the best recipe. They began not only to sell their preparations throughout Mexico, but also to export their *'chocolate real'* to Spain.

Chocolate drinking became such a popular pastime that fashionable ladies even had cups of the beverage brought to them in church. Thomas Gage tells the story of the brave Bishop of Chiapa who tried to put a stop to such sacrilege:

> The women of that city, it seems, pretend much weakness and squeamishness of stomach, which they say is so great that they are not able to continue in the church while a Mass is briefly huddled over, much less while a solemn high Mass (as they call it) is sung and a sermon preached, unless they drink a cup of hot chocolate, and eat a bit of sweetmeats to strengthen their stomachs. For this purpose it was much used by them to make their maids bring to them to church in the middle of Mass or sermon a cup of chocolate, which could not be done to all, or most of them, without a great confusion and interrupting both Mass and sermon. The Bishop perceived this abuse and gave fair warning for the omitting of it, but all without amendment. Consequently he thought fit to fix in writing upon the church's doors an excommunication against all such as should presume at the time of service to eat or drink within the church. This excommunication was taken much to heart by all,

but especially by the gentlewomen, who protested if they might not eat or drink in the church they could not continue in it ... The women ... began to stomach (be angry with) him the more and to slight him with scornful and reproachful words. Others slighted his excommunication, drinking in iniquity in the church, as the fish doth water. This caused one day such an uproar in the Cathedral that many swords were drawn against the priests and prebends, who attempted to take away from the maids the cups of chocolate which they brought unto their mistresses. These ladies seeing at last that neither fair nor foul means would prevail with the Bishop, resolved to forsake the Cathedral ... So from that time most of the city betook themselves to the cloister churches, where by the nuns and friars they were not troubled nor resisted ... This lasted not long, but the Bishop began to stomach the friars, and to set up another excommunication, binding all the city to resort unto their own cathedral church. This the women would not obey, but kept their houses for a whole month. In that time the Bishop fell dangerously sick ... Physicians were sent for far and near, who all with a joint opinion agreed that the Bishop was poisoned, and he himself doubted not of it at his death, praying unto God to forgive those that had been the cause of it ...

A gentlewoman with whom I was well acquainted in that city, who was noted to be somewhat too familiar with one of the Bishop's pages, was commonly censured. She was said to have prescribed such a cup of chocolate to be ministered by the page which poisoned him who so rigorously had forbidden chocolate to be drunk in the church. I myself heard this gentlewoman say of the deceased Bishop that she thought few grieved for him, and that she judged, he being such an enemy to chocolate in the church, that which he had drunk at home in his house had not agreed with his body. And it became afterwards a proverb in that country, 'Beware of the chocolate of Chiapa!'

LE DEJEUMER

BROYAGE

RECOLTE DES MAZORCAS DE CACAO

SECHAGE

EPLUCHAGE

COMMENT SE FAIT LE CHOCOLAT

Dessin de M. Bertrand

CHAPTER
3

COLD DESSERTS

Death by Chocolate

The good bishop of Chiapa (see page 70) was not the only victim of murder by chocolate. There is also a cautionary tale about a courtier of Louis XIII who was much devoted to the cause of improving the quality of chocolate. However, when he besmirched the honour of a lady of noble birth at the court, she invited him to drink a cup of chocolate, into which she had secretly slipped a deadly poison. Her suitor drained the cup, then drawing her to him just before he died, he whispered: 'the chocolate would have been better if you had added a little more sugar; the poison gives it a bitter flavour. Think of this the next time you offer a gentleman chocolate.'

Rumour had it that Charles II, who died in 1685, did not die of natural causes, but that his end had been brought about by his mistress, the Duchess of Portsmouth, who had offered him a cup of poisoned chocolate.

And suicide by chocolate?

> Jacob, with pistol in his hand,
> exclaims, 'Susannah, dear,
> without your love I'll kill myself?'
> Susannah quakes in fear.
> He lays the pistol to his head,
> Susannah pleads, 'Wait, wait!'
> 'Don't fret!', says Jacob, 'for this gun
> is only chocolate!'
>
> *Swiss poem, 1840*

SIMPLE CHOCOLATE MOUSSE

This is child's play to make and it never fails. If it is to be made by – or for – children, it is perfectly delicious even without alcohol. If possible, make it a day ahead so that the mixture can settle and, if you are adding spirits or liqueur, the flavour has time to mature.

175 G (6 OZ) PLAIN OR BITTER CHOCOLATE
2 TABLESPOONS BRANDY, RUM, GRAND MARNIER, CRÈME
   DE CACAO, TIA MARIA, CHOCOLATE PEPPERMINT
   LIQUEUR OR WATER
6 EGGS

Melt the chocolate with whatever liquid you are using (see page 13). Stir until smooth.

Separate the eggs and add the yolks one by one, beating in each one with a wooden spoon until well amalgamated before adding the next. The mixture will 'seize' and stiffen at first, but will gradually become soft, smooth and glossy.

Whip the egg whites until they stand in stiff peaks but are not completely dry.

Stir one third into the chocolate mixture until it is perfectly blended in, then lightly fold in the remaining whites with a spatula or spoon. Work as lightly as possible but take care that no white specks remain.

Pour into a glass or soufflé dish and refrigerate.

VARIATION: For an even smoother, richer, really velvety mousse, substitute 300 ml (½ pint) whipping cream, stiffly whipped, for the egg whites.

RICH CHOCOLATE MOUSSE

This really is rich and quite dense, and the quantity here is sufficient for six, even of the most self-indulgent.

125 G (4 OZ) PLAIN OR BITTER CHOCOLATE

2 TABLESPOONS FLAVOURING — STRONG COFFEE, RUM, BRANDY, TIA MARIA, OR ANY OTHER LIQUEUR (SEE PREVIOUS RECIPE)

75 G (3 OZ) UNSALTED BUTTER

2 EGG YOLKS

3 EGG WHITES

2 TABLESPOONS CASTER SUGAR

For decoration

1 TEASPOON COCOA POWDER, ICING SUGAR OR CHOCO-LATE FLAKES

Melt the chocolate with the flavouring (see page 13) in a large bowl and leave to cool a little.

Cut the butter into small pieces and add, a piece at a time, stirring until each is melted and fully amalgamated with the chocolate before adding the next. The chocolate and the bowl should be warm enough to melt the butter, but not so hot that the butter will turn to oil, and the mixture should have the consistency of thick cream.

Separate the eggs and stir in the yolks one by one. Make sure the mixture is quite smooth.

Whisk the egg whites until they reach the soft peak stage, then slowly add the caster sugar, continuing to whisk until they are very stiff and glossy. Fold into the chocolate mixture gently but thoroughly, making sure the two are fully blended and no white spots remain in the mousse.

Pour into a serving bowl or individual ramekin dishes and chill.

You can decorate the mousse if you like with a powdering of cocoa or icing sugar, or a sprinkling of chocolate flakes (see page 292) before serving.

NOTE: If you are using alcohol it is best to make this mousse a day in advance, to allow the flavour to mature.

CHOCOLATE MARQUISE

The richest of all the chocolate mousses, yet also the lightest, this is a party piece for accomplished cooks.

200 G (7 OZ) PLAIN OR BITTER CHOCOLATE
100 G (3½ OZ) UNSALTED BUTTER
100 G (3 OZ) CASTER SUGAR
2 TABLESPOONS COCOA POWDER
½ TEASPOON INSTANT COFFEE POWDER
3 EGG YOLKS
2 TABLESPOONS RUM OR BRANDY
300 ML (½ PINT) WHIPPING CREAM
I PACKET (18) SPONGE FINGERS OR
    3 TRIFLE SPONGES (OPTIONAL)
I TABLESPOON MILK (OPTIONAL)
I TABLESPOON VERY STRONG BLACK COFFEE (OPTIONAL)

Melt the chocolate (see page 13) and leave to cool.

Beat the butter with half the sugar until very white and fluffy. Beat in the cocoa and coffee powder.

In another bowl, whisk the yolks with remaining sugar until they are also very pale and bulky. Whisk in the rum or brandy.

Lightly whip the cream until it, too, is bulky but not stiff.

Beat the melted chocolate into the butter mixture until smooth. Pour this into the egg mixture and lightly amalgamate. Finally, fold in the cream.

You can now pour the mixture direct into a buttered ½-litre (1-pint) pudding basin or charlotte mould, or into a 500 g

(1 lb) capacity loaf tin. The unmoulding will be made easier if you line the container with foil, smoothed very straight against the sides. It is easiest to do this if you first turn the container upside down and smooth the foil into shape over the top.

The finished pudding will look more impressive still if you line the tin or mould with the sponge fingers, or the thinly sliced sponge cakes, lightly dipped in a blend of the milk and coffee, before pouring in the 'mousse' mixture.

Refrigerate for a few hours before turning out and serving.

In 1807 Napoleon took the city of Dantzig. As a gesture of friendship, he presented the governor of the vanquished city with a hundred thousand écus and a dukedom, in the guise of a tablet of chocolate; engraving, 1834

WHITE CHOCOLATE MOUSSE

Quick and simple, and refreshingly light, this must be whipped with a balloon whisk, by hand or with a powerful electric beater, in order to reach the necessary density. Make just before serving the meal and do not keep for more than about 1 hour.

100 G (3½ OZ) PLAIN OR BITTER CHOCOLATE
4 EGG WHITES
4 TABLESPOONS ICING OR CASTER SUGAR
For serving
1 TABLESPOON BRANDY OR OTHER LIQUEUR (OPTIONAL)
SINGLE CREAM (OPTIONAL)

Grate the chocolate very finely.

Whip the egg whites until they stand in soft peaks, then whisk in the sugar until the mixture is very stiff and glossy. Fold in the grated chocolate.

Pour into individual bowls or serving glasses.

You can pour a little brandy, liqueur or cream round the edges just before serving.

NOTE: You can also blend a little powdered cinnamon with the caster sugar.

COMPAGNIE FRANÇAISE DES CHOCOLATS ET DES THÈS

PETITS POTS AU CHOCOLAT
Individual Chocolate Creams

One of the simplest of the chocolate desserts, especially if you have an electric blender.

200 G (7 OZ) PLAIN OR BITTER CHOCOLATE
300 ML (½ PINT) SINGLE CREAM
DASH OF SALT
3–4 DROPS VANILLA ESSENCE
1 EGG

If using a blender, break the chocolate into the blender jar.

Scald the cream and, when just boiling, pour on to the chocolate and blend till smooth. Blend in the salt and vanilla and the whole egg.

If you do not have a blender, scald the cream, take it off the heat and add the chocolate. Leave for 5 minutes for the chocolate to melt, then stir till smooth. Add the salt, the vanilla and the egg lightly beaten with a fork to amalgamate. Beat over a very gentle heat with a wooden spoon until absolutely smooth.

Pour into four to six individual pots or ramekin dishes and chill for at least 3–4 hours before serving. The mixture will set to a thick, smooth cream.

CHOCOLATE BAVARIAN CREAM

A very light, elegant dessert.

100 G (3½ OZ) PLAIN OR BITTER CHOCOLATE
SCANT ½ LITRE (¾ PINT) MILK
15 G (½ OZ) GELATINE
150 ML (¼ PINT) VERY STRONG BLACK COFFEE
5 EGGS
150 G (5 OZ) CASTER SUGAR
½ TEASPOON CORNFLOUR
2 TABLESPOONS RUM, BRANDY OR ORANGE LIQUEUR
    (OPTIONAL)
2 TABLESPOONS PRALINE, SEE PAGE 20 (OPTIONAL)
150 ML (¼ PINT) DOUBLE OR WHIPPING CREAM
For decoration (optional)
75 ML (⅛ PINT) WHIPPING CREAM
25 G (I OZ) PLAIN OR BITTER CHOCOLATE

Break the chocolate into the milk and heat together slowly, stirring until the chocolate has melted, then boil gently for 3 minutes so that the mixture becomes really smooth.

Sprinkle the gelatine over the coffee and leave to soak.

Separate the eggs and beat the yolks with half the sugar and the cornflour until very thick and creamy. Slowly pour on the hot chocolate milk, blend well, then return to the pan and stir over a gentle heat until the mixture begins to thicken and just coats the back of the spoon. Do not allow it to boil. Remove from the heat.

Heat the soaked gelatine for a few moments to dissolve,

then stir into the hot chocolate custard. Add rum, brandy or liqueur or praline. Set aside to cool.

When the custard has cooled but not begun to set, whisk the egg whites until they begin to stand in peaks, then whisk in the remaining sugar. Fold into the custard.

Whip the cream lightly and also fold it in. Pour the finished cream into a serving dish and leave to set in the refrigerator for at least 2 hours.

You can decorate with rosettes of whipped cream and grated chocolate or chocolate curls (see page 292) before serving.

'*Confiseur*', from Diderot and d'Alembert, *Encyclopédie*, 1763

CHOCOLATE MOULD

A very good children's dessert.

175 G (6 OZ) PLAIN OR BITTER CHOCOLATE
15 G (½ OZ) GELATINE
2 TABLESPOONS VERY STRONG BLACK COFFEE
4 LARGE EGGS
175 G (6 OZ) SUGAR
300 ML (½ PINT) DOUBLE OR WHIPPING CREAM
For serving
150 ML (¼ PINT) DOUBLE OR WHIPPING CREAM
    OR 300 ML (½ PINT) CUSTARD
2 TABLESPOONS RUM (OPTIONAL)

Melt the chocolate (see page 13) and leave to cool.

Sprinkle the gelatine on to the coffee and leave to soak for 5 minutes, then heat gently until it has completely dissolved. Leave to cool.

Whisk the whole eggs with the sugar until they are thick and spongy and have at least trebled in volume.

Whip the cream until thick but not stiff, then whisk in the cooled melted chocolate.

Combine the two mixtures and gently blend in the gelatine, preferably with a balloon whisk, so that it is evenly distributed.

Rinse a ring mould with cold water, then pour in the mixture. Leave in the refrigerator till set.

Before serving, whip the cream lightly and blend in the

rum. Turn the mould out on to a serving dish and fill the centre with the cream.

Alternatively you can serve the dessert with a good home-made custard, into which you may also blend the rum.

CHOCOLATE CARAMEL CREAM

A pleasant, uncloying variation on a familiar dessert.

100 G (3½ OZ) SUGAR
300 ML (1 PINT) MILK
100 G (3½ OZ) PLAIN OR BITTER CHOCOLATE
1 TEASPOON INSTANT COFFEE POWDER (OPTIONAL)
3 LARGE EGGS OR 2 WHOLE EGGS AND 2 YOLKS

Melt all but one tablespoon of the sugar in a small heavy-based pan until it caramelizes to a deep gold colour. Pour it immediately into a 1-litre (2-pint) ovenproof dish with rounded sides, and turn the dish about so that the entire base and at least the first inch of the sides are covered. Leave to set.

Set the oven at gas mark 4 (180°C) 350°F.

Bring the milk to the boil and, as soon as it has boiled, remove it from the heat and add the chocolate and the coffee powder. Stir until the chocolate has melted and is thoroughly blended with the milk.

Beat the eggs and yolks together briefly in a bowl with the remaining sugar, using a fork or hand whisk. Pour on the hot chocolate milk and stir till blended.

Strain the chocolate custard mixture through a nylon sieve into the ovenproof dish. Set it in a roasting tin with enough hot water to come half-way up the sides of the dish and cook in the oven for 45 minutes to 1 hour, or until the custard has set. Test by inserting the point of a knife into the centre — it will come out clean when the cream is set.

You may cook it in a lower oven for longer if you wish, but do not set it in a hotter oven, or the custard will boil, produce bubbles and become leathery.

Remove from the oven when set and leave to cool, then refrigerate.

Run a knife round the edge and turn out into a deep dish before serving, taking care not to spill any of the syrup. If the caramel has not all dissolved, chisel it off the bottom of the dish with a knife and arrange on top of the cream – a piece of crunchy toffee is a prize!

'OLD ENGLISH' CHOCOLATE FLAN

Eat this delicate flan within hours of making and there will be a wonderful contrast between the crisp casing and meltingly light filling – but it may be a little difficult to slice it tidily. Leave it till the following day and the crust will have become soft and the filling thick and fudgy – just as delicious in a very different way.

For the flan case
175 G (6 OZ) GROUND ALMONDS
50 G (2 OZ) CASTER SUGAR
1 EGG WHITE

For the filling
300 ML (½ PINT) SINGLE CREAM
225 G (8 OZ) PLAIN OR BITTER CHOCOLATE

For decoration (OPTIONAL)
150 ML (¼ PINT) WHIPPING CREAM
CHOCOLATE FLAKES (SEE PAGE 292)

Blend the almonds and sugar together thoroughly, then mix to a smooth paste with the egg white. Gather into a ball and leave to rest for 1 hour in the refrigerator.

Set the oven at gas mark 4 (180°C) 350°F.

Roll out the pastry on a lightly floured board and line a 23 cm (9 in) diameter flan case. This pastry is very fragile, and you may need to do a little patchwork.

Bake in the centre of the oven for 30 minutes.

Remove from the oven, leave to cool and harden a little for 10–15 minutes; then, unless you used a flan ring on a baking sheet, release by gently bending the tin until the pastry case springs loose. Leave on a wire rack to finish cooling.

To make the filling, pour the cream into a small, heavy saucepan, break in the chocolate and stir over a gentle heat until the chocolate has melted and the sauce is completely smooth. Remove from the heat, set the pan in a bowl of cold water and continue to beat with a wooden spoon until the cream is cold. Pour into the flan case – it will set quite quickly.

You can decorate the flan before serving by piping on little whirls of whipped cream and sprinkling them with chocolate flakes.

KENTUCKY CHOCOLATE PIE

Rich and fudgy, but to make it even fudgier, use soft brown sugar.

225 G (8 OZ) SHORTCRUST PASTRY
300 ML (½ PINT) SINGLE CREAM
50 G (2 OZ) PLAIN OR BITTER CHOCOLATE
225 G (8 OZ) SUGAR
2 TABLESPOONS CORNFLOUR
2 TABLESPOONS WATER
2 EGGS
½ TEASPOON VANILLA ESSENCE
I TABLESPOON RUM
50 G (2 OZ) BUTTER, CUT IN SMALL PIECES

For decoration (optional)
150 ML (¼ PINT) WHIPPING CREAM
CHOCOLATE FLAKES (SEE PAGE 292)

Set the oven at gas mark 6 (200°C) 400°F.

Line a 23 cm (9 in) diameter flan case with the pastry, prick it all over with a fork and bake blind for 20–25 minutes, until it is crisp and light golden brown. Leave to cool.

Put the cream, the chocolate and the sugar in a heavy saucepan and stir over a low heat until the chocolate and sugar have melted.

Stir the cornflour and water together to make a smooth paste.

Beat the eggs together lightly.

Add the cornflour mixture and the eggs to the saucepan, and stir continually over low heat for about 10 minutes. On no account allow the mixture to boil, but it should become very thick and smooth and, when ready, it should not taste in the least floury.

Remove from the heat, stir in the vanilla essence and the rum and beat in the butter.

Pour into the baked pastry shell and leave to chill.

Decorate with the whipped cream and chocolate flakes if you like before serving.

CHOCOLATE CHIFFON PIE

Lighter than the Kentucky Chocolate Pie and very velvety.

225 G (8 OZ) SHORTCRUST PASTRY
10 G (SCANT ½ OZ) GELATINE
2 TABLESPOONS WATER
300 ML (½ PINT) MILK
85 G (3 OZ) PLAIN OR BITTER CHOCOLATE
3 EGGS
100 G (4 OZ) SUGAR
½ TEASPOON VANILLA ESSENCE
PINCH OF SALT
150 ML (¼ PINT) WHIPPING CREAM (OPTIONAL)

Set the oven at gas mark 6 (200°C) 400°F.

Line a 23 cm (9 in) diameter flan case with the pastry, prick it all over with a fork and bake blind for 20–25 minutes until it is crisp and light golden brown. Leave to cool.

Sprinkle the gelatine into the water and leave to soften.

Heat the milk in a small, heavy saucepan, add the chocolate and stir until the chocolate has dissolved. Bring to just below boiling point.

Separate the eggs and beat the yolks lightly with all but 2 tablespoons of the sugar, then blend in a little of the hot chocolate milk. Return to the milk in the saucepan, add the vanilla and stir over a low heat until the custard begins to thicken. Do not allow to boil.

Remove from the heat, add the gelatine and stir until it has completely dissolved. Leave to cool.

When the mixture has cooled and begins to set, whip the egg whites with the pinch of salt until they stand in soft peaks. Add remaining sugar and beat until they are stiff. Fold into the chocolate custard. Pour into the pastry case and chill until set.

Decorate with whipped cream if you like before serving.

VARIATION: To make CHOCOLATE RUM CHIFFON PIE, make the custard without adding the chocolate to the milk.

After stirring in the gelatine, divide the custard in half and add 50 g (2 oz) chocolate, broken into small pieces, to one half, stirring until it has melted and the custard is quite smooth.

Add 1 tablespoon rum to the other half of the custard.

Fold half the whipped egg whites into each custard when cooled, then pour the chocolate mixture first into the pastry case. Smooth over the top and pour over the rum mixture evenly to cover.

They will set in two distinct layers, so that the chocolate comes as a surprise when you cut the pie, and the rum adds an extra kick.

For a marbled effect (see cover) let the two custards nearly set, then pour into the pastry shell in alternate strips. Swirl together with a two-pronged fork or spatula.

CHOCOLATE NUT FUDGE PIE

Nicest made with a mixture of different nuts, but this delightfully chewy pie can be made with any one kind of nut only.

175 G (6 OZ) SHORTCRUST PASTRY
275 G (10 OZ) SOFT BROWN SUGAR
150 ML (¼ PINT) WATER
125 G (4 OZ) UNSALTED BUTTER
225 G (8 OZ) NUTS – ALMONDS, HAZELNUTS, WALNUTS,
   PECANS OR BRAZILS (SHELLED WEIGHT)
150 ML (¼ PINT) DOUBLE CREAM
50 G (2 OZ) PLAIN OR BITTER CHOCOLATE

Set the oven at gas mark 5 (190°C) 375°F.

Roll out the pastry, line a 20 cm (8 in) diameter flan case with it, prick it all over with a fork and bake blind for 20–25 minutes, or until pale brown and fully cooked. Remove from the oven and leave to cool.

Meanwhile, put the sugar and water into a saucepan and bring slowly to the boil, stirring well until the sugar has dissolved. Boil till it reaches 122°C (250°F) on a sugar thermometer, or until a small amount of the mixture dropped into cold water forms a hard ball. Remove from the heat and add the butter cut in pieces. Stir until smooth.

Add the nuts and all but one dessertspoon of the cream, return to the heat and bring gently to the boil. Lower the heat and leave to simmer for 10–15 minutes.

When the mixture looks quite thick, remove from the heat, leave to cool a little, then pour into the pastry case.

Melt the chocolate (see page 13), add the remaining cream and stir until smooth.

Smooth over the top of the butterscotch and leave in a cool place to set before serving.

CHOCOLATE YOGURT AMBROSIA

Refreshing and very quick and simple to make.

300 ML ($\frac{1}{2}$ PINT) PLAIN YOGURT
300 ML ($\frac{1}{2}$ PINT) DOUBLE CREAM
25 G (1 OZ) PLAIN OR BITTER CHOCOLATE
6–8 TEASPOONS SOFT BROWN SUGAR (OR MORE)

Whip the yogurt and cream together until the mixture becomes light and quite thick.

Grate the chocolate finely and blend in.

Pour into six or eight individual ramekin dishes and sprinkle each dish with a teaspoon of soft brown sugar.

Refrigerate for several hours or overnight. The mixture will have set like a junket, and the sugar will have dissolved into a rich brown syrup.

Sprinkle on a little more sugar before serving, if you wish.

SICILIAN CASSATA

The real Sicilian cassata is not a many-layered ice cream confection, but a much more delicate blend of ricotta cheese with fruit and chocolate, encased in light sponge and covered with a thick coating of dark, smooth chocolate icing. It is a sensational dish for a special occasion.

By rights a cassata should be made in a rounded *bombe* mould or pudding basin, but it is easier, at any rate the first time, to make it in a loaf tin.

Ricotta is not easily obtained in England, and when you can get it, it is often not as fresh as is necessary for this dessert. Unless your ricotta is very moist and fresh, it is better to use a blend, half and half, of ricotta and curd cheese. If necessary, you can use curd cheese only.

500 G (I LB) RICOTTA OR CURD CHEESE (SEE ABOVE)
50 G (2 OZ) SUGAR
4 TABLESPOONS STREGA OR GRAND MARNIER OR ORANGE
   CURAÇAO
100 G (4 OZ) MIXED CANDIED PEEL
50 G (2 OZ) PLAIN OR BITTER CHOCOLATE OR CHOCOLATE
   CHIPS
6–8 SQUARES TRIFLE SPONGE
For the icing
175 G (6 OZ) PLAIN OR BITTER CHOCOLATE
3 TABLESPOONS STRONG BLACK COFFEE
75 G (3 OZ) UNSALTED BUTTER

Blend the cheese with the sugar and half the liqueur and whisk until the mixture becomes light and smooth.

Chop the candied peel quite small, but so that the pieces remain distinct, and chop the chocolate into similar size pieces if you are not using chocolate chips. Fold both into the cheese.

Split the sponge squares in half across the middle and dribble some of the remaining liqueur over the cut surface of each square.

Line a 1-litre (2-pint) *bombe* mould or pudding basin, or a loaf tin, with foil. (It is easiest to do this if you turn the mould or tin upside down and smooth the foil over it first.) Line it with the sponge, cut side inwards, and fill with the cheese mixture. Lay the last pieces of sponge over the top.

Place a piece of foil over the top and refrigerate for a few hours at least, preferably overnight, so that the filling becomes firm.

Ice the cake at least one hour before serving.

Melt the chocolate with the coffee (see page 13). Cut the butter into small pieces and blend them into the chocolate one at a time, stirring each time to amalgamate before adding the next.

Allow the icing to cool a little, then turn the cassata out on to a dish and spread the icing over it generously. If there is too much for one coating, refrigerate for half an hour to allow the first coat to set and then spread on the remaining icing. Leave to set for at least one hour before serving.

NOTE: For a simpler version of this dessert, make the filling only and serve it with sponge fingers or wafer biscuits.

CREAM CHEESE AND COCOA

The Italians have a marvellously simple dessert called *ricotta al caffè* which consists of mounds of ricotta or curd cheese, some freshly ground coffee, sugar and rum or brandy. It is just as good with cocoa instead of coffee, but the cocoa should be a really good quality, 'pure' cocoa to get the delicately bitter flavour.

The ricotta must be very fresh and moist – if not, it is better to use curd cheese.

This dessert is deceptively rich, and though these quantities may not seem very great, they should be ample for four.

250 G (8 OZ) RICOTTA OR CURD CHEESE (SEE ABOVE)
4 TABLESPOONS 'PURE' COCOA POWDER
4 DESSERTSPOONS SUGAR
4 DESSERTSPOONS RUM OR BRANDY

Pass the ricotta or curd cheese through a nylon sieve or whisk it briefly to make it smooth, then put a mound on each plate.

Add a little heap of cocoa and one of sugar separately on the plates, and dribble the rum or brandy over the cheese.

Everyone then dips each spoonful of cheese first into the cocoa and then into the sugar.

GÖTTERSPEISE
Food of the Gods

A good way to use up any cranberries or cranberry sauce left over from Christmas. This quickly assembled dessert is very rich and these quantities, which may not seem very much, are sufficient for four to six.

250 G (8 OZ) CRANBERRIES
2 TABLESPOONS WATER
75 G (3 OZ) SUGAR
125 G (4 OZ) PUMPERNICKEL
150 ML ($\frac{1}{4}$ PINT) WHIPPING CREAM
1 TABLESPOON CASTER OR ICING SUGAR
50 G (2 OZ) PLAIN OR BITTER CHOCOLATE

Cook the cranberries till just soft with the water and sugar. Leave to cool.

Reduce the pumpernickel to fine crumbs. This can be done in a food processor, or you can grate the pumpernickel quite easily if you keep it together in the block.

Make a layer of the pumpernickel in the bottom of a glass dish and spread on the cranberries.

Whip the cream lightly with the caster or icing sugar and spread over the top.

Sprinkle the finely chopped chocolate over the top – do not grate it, as it should be slightly crunchy.

NOTE: For an even more special effect add half an unpeeled orange, sliced then chopped (peel and all) to the cranberries as soon as they come off the heat.

You can also add some finely chopped pecans or walnuts.

CHOCOLATE REFRIGERATOR CAKE

Refrigerator cakes are quick and easy to make and require no cooking. They freeze extremely well and are a useful standby.

While this will never be exactly a plain dessert, you can make it more or less luxurious, according to whether you use digestive or tea biscuits, sponge fingers, or – the ultimate luxury – some good, hard Italian macaroons. The brandy is of course optional, although I would hate to leave it out. The milk is only necessary with sponge fingers, which otherwise remain too dry.

250 G (8 OZ) PLAIN OR BITTER CHOCOLATE
3 TABLESPOONS VERY STRONG BLACK COFFEE
250 G (8 OZ) UNSALTED BUTTER
200 G (6 OZ) SUGAR
I TABLESPOON COCOA
3 EGGS
APPROX. 250 G (8 OZ) BISCUITS (SEE ABOVE)
2–3 TABLESPOONS BRANDY (OPTIONAL)
2–3 TABLESPOONS MILK (OPTIONAL) SEE ABOVE

Melt the chocolate with the coffee (see page 13) and leave to cool.

Whisk the butter with the sugar until light and fluffy, then whisk in the cocoa. Separate the eggs and beat in the yolks one by one.

Blend the melted chocolate into the mixture.

Whisk the whites until they stand in stiff peaks and fold gently but thoroughly into the chocolate cream.

Line a 23–25 cm (9–10 in) diameter loose-bottomed cake tin with foil. If you are using digestive or tea biscuits, break them up roughly and make a first layer on the bottom of the tin. If you are using macaroons, lay them in a single layer on the bottom. Dribble on a little of the brandy.

If you are using sponge fingers, blend the milk and the brandy in a saucer and briefly dip in each finger before using them to line the bottom of the tin.

Spread a thick layer of the chocolate cream over the biscuits, and then repeat until everything has been used up.

Refrigerate overnight, or freeze for about 2 hours before turning out and serving.

NOTE: To make it even richer, fold 50 g (2 oz) chopped walnuts and/or 50 g (2 oz) chopped glacé cherries into the chocolate cream.

CHOCOLATE PRALINE DIPLOMATE

This is a wonderful party dessert. There is no problem whatever about making a very large *diplomate*; it is simple to prepare, looks and tastes wonderful, and you can serve it fresh or frozen. Indeed, I have sometimes made two and put one in the freezer in the hope that it may live to fight another day, but when the first proved too popular, I have taken the second out and served it straight from the freezer.

It is equally good made with an almond or a hazelnut praline.

100 G (4 OZ) ALMONDS OR HAZELNUTS
75 G (3 OZ) SUGAR
50 G (2 OZ) PLAIN OR BITTER CHOCOLATE
300 ML (½ PINT) DOUBLE CREAM
150 ML (¼ PINT) SINGLE CREAM
I TABLESPOON CASTER SUGAR
I TABLESPOON VERY STRONG BLACK COFFEE
I TABLESPOON TIA MARIA (OR ANY OTHER LIQUEUR)
I TABLESPOON BRANDY
I TABLESPOON TOP OF THE MILK
3 PACKETS OF (18) SPONGE FINGERS

Make a fairly coarse praline with the nuts and sugar as described on page 20.

Melt the chocolate (see page 13) and leave to cool.

Put the two creams and the sugar into a large bowl together and whip with a balloon whisk until the mixture is bulky but very light. Blend in the cooled chocolate.

Blend the coffee, liqueur, brandy and top of the milk together in a small bowl or saucer. Dip some sponge fingers, one by one, very quickly into the mixture on the plain side, and make a layer very close together in the bottom of a large springform mould or flan dish or tin, 25 cm (10 in) minimum diameter. Cover this layer with half the chocolate cream, spread over smoothly and sprinkle on half the praline. Make a second layer with the remaining fingers and cream, and sprinkle a thick layer of praline on top.

Refrigerate for a few hours before serving, or freeze (see above).

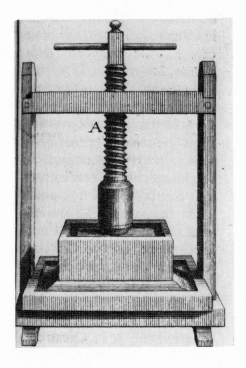

Early cocoa press

CHOCOLATE PAVLOVA

Although sinfully rich, this dessert is also very light, and the cinnamon, which may be omitted from the meringue mixture but should certainly be whipped into the cream, adds a welcome grace note of bitterness.

For the meringue
6 EGG WHITES
PINCH OF SALT
350 G (12 OZ) CASTER SUGAR
½ TEASPOON GROUND CINNAMON (OPTIONAL)
For the filling
200 G (7 OZ) PLAIN OR BITTER CHOCOLATE
4 TABLESPOONS WATER OR BRANDY
4 EGG YOLKS
For the topping
300 ML (½ PINT) DOUBLE OR WHIPPING CREAM
I TEASPOON CASTER SUGAR
½ TEASPOON GROUND CINNAMON

Set the oven at gas mark 2 (150°C) 300°F.

Prepare a 30 cm (12 in) square or round baking sheet. Line it with foil, butter the foil generously and powder with flour. Knock off excess flour.

Whisk the egg whites with the salt until they begin to stand in peaks, then slowly whisk in half the sugar. Continue to whisk until the mixture is very stiff, white and opaque, then quickly fold in remaining sugar, into which you may blend the cinnamon.

Pipe or spread the meringue mixture in a 25 cm (10 in) diameter circle on the baking sheet. If you are using a piping bag, use a 1 cm ($\frac{1}{2}$ in) nozzle and pipe two thick extra rings around the perimeter to form a raised edge. If you are spreading the mixture with a palette knife, spread it more thickly towards the edges, to form a kind of nest shape. Dust with a little caster sugar to form a light crust.

Bake for half an hour, then lower the oven to gas mark $\frac{1}{2}$ (120°C) 250°F, and cook for 1–1$\frac{1}{2}$ hours, depending on how dry you like your meringue. The meringue should have risen a little, have a light crust on the outside, and can afford to be just soft in the centre.

When cooked, allow to cool a little, then lift off the baking sheet and peel off the foil. If the base of the meringue is sticky or soft, place upside down on the baking sheet and return to the oven for a further 15–30 minutes to dry off. Leave on a wire tray to cool.

Prepare the filling while the meringue is cooking.

Melt the chocolate with the water or brandy (see page 13) and stir until smooth. Blend in the egg yolks one by one and cook over simmering water, stirring all the time, until the mixture lightly thickens. Leave to cool.

When the meringue is ready, and not more than an hour or so before serving, spread the chocolate cream into the centre of the meringue.

Whip the cream lightly with the sugar blended with the cinnamon until it stands in soft peaks.

Spread over the top of the entire pavlova, and decorate with a further sprinkling of cinnamon or some chocolate curls (see page 292) or coarsely grated chocolate.

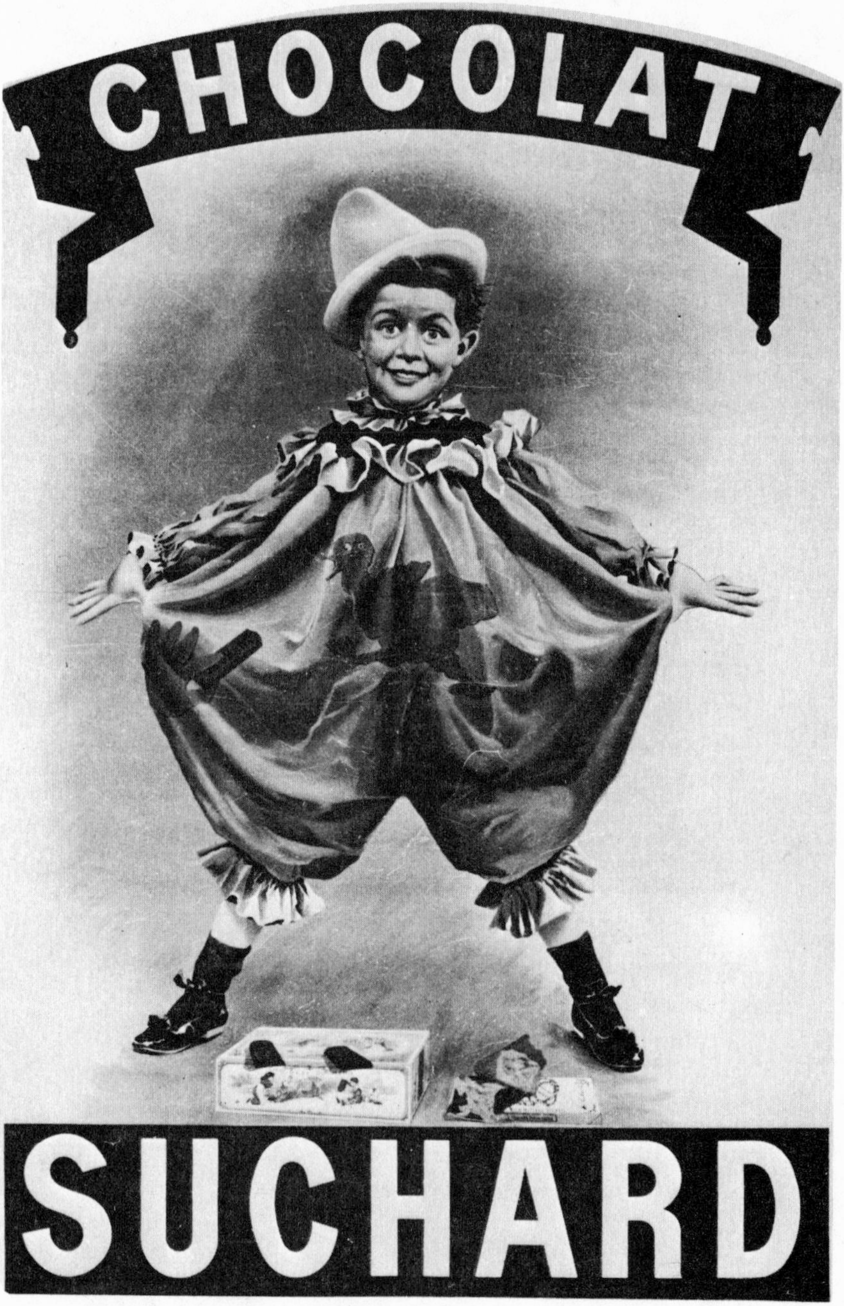
CHOCOLAT
SUCHARD

PEARS BELLE HÉLÈNE

This dish (created by the great Escoffier and probably named after one of the most desired women the world has ever known) is a delectable combination of pears with ice cream and chocolate sauce. The ice cream should preferably be home-made, or the best quality bought, and there are a number of other embellishments that can be added.

6 RIPE EATING PEARS (I PER PERSON)
50 G (2 OZ APPROX.) SUGAR
I VANILLA POD
¾ LITRE (I½ PINTS) VANILLA ICE CREAM (SEE ABOVE)

For the chocolate sauce
100 G (4 OZ) PLAIN OR BITTER CHOCOLATE
300 ML (½ PINT) WATER
50 G (2 OZ) UNSALTED BUTTER

For decoration (optional)
50 G (2 OZ) FLAKED TOASTED ALMONDS OR 2 TABLESPOONS
    PRALINE POWDER (SEE PAGE 20)

Peel and core the pears but leave them whole. They should be ripe but firm, and the exact quantity of sugar needed will depend on the sweetness of the pears.

Choose a saucepan that is just large enough for the pears to stand upright side by side, and put in enough water to cover them but do not put in the pears for the moment. Add sugar and vanilla to the water, bring to the boil and simmer for 5 minutes, then add the pears and poach them until they are tender, but do not allow them to disintegrate.

Leave the pears to cool in the syrup.

Prepare the chocolate sauce by putting the chocolate and water into a heavy saucepan and heating slowly, stirring until the chocolate has melted and the mixture is smooth.

When you are ready to serve the dessert, put the ice cream into one large serving dish or 6 individual ones. Place the lightly drained pears on top.

Have the chocolate sauce almost at boiling point, remove from the heat and add the butter cut into small pieces, one at a time. Stir quickly until all the butter has melted and the sauce is smooth and glossy. Pour over the pears and serve very quickly. You may sprinkle with toasted flaked almonds or praline powder just before serving.

VARIATION: The dish can be made more elaborate and even more delicious by stuffing the pears with chocolate macaroons (see page 238), or the cream can be set on a base of sponge cake soaked with a mixture of the pear syrup and kirsch, or Poire William liqueur.

PEARS BELLE PHYLLIS Another variation on the same theme, deceptively simple to make but very sophisticated.

Peel and core some good eating pears, cut them into small pieces and poach these in the minimum of water until quite soft.

Puree with a fork or in a blender and add Poire William liqueur or sugar to taste. Serve warm, sprinkled with plenty of coarsely grated plain or bitter chocolate. The chocolate will melt deliciously as you eat.

WHY 'COCOA' AND WHY 'CHOCOLATE'

When the Spaniards were first introduced to cocoa they learnt the word the Mexicans used, which was *cacao*. They brought the word as well as the bean home with them, and in every other European language that is still the word – except in English. It seems that this particular combination of sounds proved too difficult for English tongues, and they twisted it to *cocoa*, which it has remained ever since.

The derivation of the word *chocolate* is a little less clear. Some authorities, among them Thomas Gage, who first wrote of chocolate in English, thought that 'the name is compounded from *atte*, as some say, or as other, *atle*, which in the Mexican language signifieth water, and from the sound which the water (wherein is put the Chocolate) makes, choco, choco, choco, when it is stirred in a cup by an instrument called a *molinet*, or *molinillo*, until it bubble and rise unto a froath.'

Other authorities believe the Aztec word *xocoatl* was from the Nahuatl word meaning 'bitter water' – certainly an apt description of the beverage as the Aztecs drank it.

DU
CHOCOLATE
DISCOVRS CVRIEVX,
DIVISE' EN QUATRE
PARTIES

Par Antoine Colmenero de Ledesma
Medecin & Chirurgien de la Ville
de Ecija de l'Andalouzie.

Traduit d'Espagnol en François
sur l'Impression faite à Madrid
l'an 1631. & éclaircy de quel-
ques Annotations,

Par RENE' MOREAV *Professeur*
du Roy en Medecine à Paris.

Plus est adjoûté vn Dialogue touchant
le même Chocolate.

CHOCOLATE SPREADS ACROSS EUROPE

The Spanish chocolate monopoly was finally broken when an Italian visitor to Spain, one Antonio Carletti, took the recipe for the drink back to Italy in 1606. A century later, and the coffee houses of Florence and Venice were famous throughout Europe for their chocolate, although even then it was only the fashionable ladies who drank it, while their maids, like Despina in Mozart's *Così fan Tutte*, had to beat the chocolate for half an hour, and then all they were allowed to do was to smell it.

Meanwhile, France had already been introduced to chocolate in the sixteenth century by the Jews, driven out of Spain, who had settled near Bayonne (still a chocolate-making area today). But the exotic drink did not spread beyond this south-west corner of France, and in 1651 when Anne of Austria, daughter of the King of Spain, married Louis XIII of France, she not only brought her own chocolate with her, but also a special maid, La Molina, to prepare it. She drank her chocolate only in private, with her closest friends and intimates, but her niece, Maria Theresa, who married Louis XIV forty-five years later, was so infatuated with it that she presented her future husband with chocolate in an ornate casket as an engagement gift. It was said of her that 'chocolate and the King are her only passions' (note the order), and chocolate immediately became the rage at court.

Fashion is fickle, however, and chocolate went in and out of favour with amazing rapidity. Since this period saw the birth of the café (the first of which – the Café Procope in Paris – was later patronized by, among others, Diderot, Napoleon and Verlaine, and still survives today as a flourishing restaurant), the drinking of chocolate was beginning to spread among the less affluent, and consequently its popularity began to decline at court.

Mme de Sévigné, that indefatigable correspondent, chronicles its fortunes, declaring at one time that 'like Racine, it would go out of fashion very quickly', and at another reporting that, at the threat of an impending shortage due to a disease of the tree and hurricanes in the Antilles, the Duke of Alba had laid in two years' supply. The question of whether it was fashionable or not, let alone good for you, caused her continual anxiety. On 15 April 1671 she writes to her daughter:

And now, my dear child, I must tell you that chocolate no longer holds the place in my esteem that it used to do; fashion has influenced me, as it always does; those who used to praise chocolate, now speak ill of it, revile it, and accuse it of all the disorders to which we are subject. It occasions the vapours, and palpitation of the heart; it flatters you for a time indeed, but presently lights up a fever that continues, and at length carries you to the grave. In short, my dear, the grand master, who used to live upon it, is become its declared enemy; judge then, if I can be its friend. Let me entreat you no longer to be an advocate for it, for it is no longer in fashion with the genteel part of the world.

Only a few months later, on 28 October, she reinstated chocolate in her favour:

I had a mind to be friends again with chocolate, and so took some the day before yesterday, by way of digesting my dinner, that I

Chocolate and a love letter served in the bath; 'The Bath' by Freudeberg

might make the better supper; and yesterday took some again by
way of nourishment, to enable me to fast till supper-time: it had
every way the desired effect: and what I think very extraordinary
is, that it acted according to my wishes.

At times (tongue in cheek?) she attributes to it quite remarkable powers: 'The Marquise de C took too much
chocolate being pregnant last year, that she was brought to
bed of a little boy who was as black as the devil.'

Whether it was in royal favour or not, chocolate had
certainly come to stay. On 20 May 1659 Louis XIV granted
a royal warrant to *'notre cher et bien aimé'* David Chaliou, of
the rue St Honoré, *'de faire vendre et débiter dans toutes les villes
et autres lieux du royaume, une certaine composition qui se nomme
chocolat'*; by 1692 the letters patent had passed to François
Dumaine, specifying that the price of cocoa may not exceed
4 francs a pound, and in March 1693 the privilege was
abolished altogether and the sale of chocolate became free.

In Germany, chocolate began to make its appearance
towards the end of the seventeenth century, and in 1704
Frederick I of Prussia imposed a duty of two thaler on anyone
wishing to enjoy the drink. In 1747, Frederick the Great
forbade all public hawking, especially that of chocolate.
While by no means averse to enjoying a good cup of chocolate himself with his friend Voltaire, and sometimes sending
a tablet of the precious substance to his favoured generals, the
frugal Frederick commissioned a chemist to produce a substitute made from lime leaves. Not surprisingly, it failed
to catch on. In a neighbouring state, Prince Wilhelm
von Schaumburg-Lippe founded a chocolate factory in
Steinhude in 1756, using Portuguese labour to ensure high
quality, and soon chocolate factories blossomed everywhere.

Austria was initiated into chocolate-drinking by Charles

VI, when he brought his court from Madrid in 1711, although itinerant monks had probably introduced it earlier, at least to the monasteries.

The first mention of chocolate in Switzerland, now the chocolate capital of Europe, comes in 1697, when Heinrich Escher, a mayor of Zurich, brought word of the new drink on his return from a visit to Brussels.

*   *   *   *   *   *   *   *   *

'When I die,' I said to my friend, 'I'm not going to be embalmed, I'm going to be dipped.'

'Milk chocolate or bittersweet?' was her immediate concern.

This is the rhetorical response of one chocolate addict to another. We both know the answer. Bittersweet.

From *The Chocolate Bible* by Adrianne Marcus

*   *   *   *   *   *   *   *   *

CHAPTER
4

FROZEN DESSERTS

CHOCOLATE SORBET

Dark, smooth and very economical; the cinnamon adds an extra depth to the flavour and a little lightly whipped, rum- or liqueur-laced cream makes an excellent accompaniment.

200 G (7 OZ) SUGAR
50 G (2 OZ) COCOA POWDER
PINCH OF SALT
1 TEASPOON INSTANT COFFEE POWDER
1 STICK CINNAMON OR ¼ TEASPOON GROUND CINNAMON
600 ML (1 PINT) WATER
For serving (optional)
150 ML (¼ PINT) WHIPPING CREAM
2 TEASPOONS SUGAR
½ TABLESPOON RUM, CRÈME DE CACAO OR TIA MARIA

Put all the main ingredients into a heavy saucepan in the order listed and bring very slowly to the boil, stirring until the sugar has dissolved and the liquid in the pan is completely smooth.

Keep the mixture boiling very gently for 5 minutes, stirring from time to time and making quite sure that it neither sticks to the bottom nor boils over. Then remove it from the heat and leave to cool.

Strain into an ice cream maker or a metal container. If you are using an ice cream maker, follow the manufacturer's instructions. Otherwise set into the freezing compartment of the refrigerator or the fast-freeze section of the freezer until firmly frozen (2–3 hours). Remove from the refrigerator, put the sorbet into a chilled blender or food processor and process until completely smooth.

Return to freeze for at least another hour.

Serve straight from frozen into chilled bowls or glasses. Top, if you wish, with a good dollop of the cream, lightly whipped with the sugar and rum or liqueur, or pour the liqueur over separately.

ECONOMICAL CHOCOLATE ICE CREAM

This is the least rich of the ice creams, but it has a good chocolaty taste, a smooth texture and dark colour. Serve plain or with whipped cream, or sprinkled with chopped nuts or praline (see page 20). This is also the best ice to use with meringues or in such dishes as *bombes*, Baked Alaska or Chocolat Liégeois.

To give added depth of flavour, also try making this ice with brown sugar.

300 ML (½ PINT) MILK
125 G (4 OZ) PLAIN OR BITTER CHOCOLATE
3 EGG YOLKS
50 G (2 OZ) SUGAR

Scald the milk, then remove from the heat and add the chocolate. Leave to melt and then stir until smooth.

Meanwhile whisk the yolks with the sugar until pale and thick, then slowly whisk in the chocolate milk.

Return to the saucepan and stir over a gentle heat until the mixture thickens.

Pour into a freezing tray or serving dish and freeze.

Remove from the freezer 1 hour before serving and store in the refrigerator.

RICH CHOCOLATE ICE CREAM

This is a good creamy ice, smooth and rich but not cloying, and you can vary the amount of whipped cream you add to suit your taste. This ice is particularly good sprinkled with a thick layer of chopped hazelnuts or toasted almonds before serving.

300 ML ($\frac{1}{2}$ PINT) SINGLE CREAM OR MILK
125 G (4 OZ) PLAIN OR BITTER CHOCOLATE
2 TEASPOONS INSTANT COFFEE POWDER (OPTIONAL)
4 EGG YOLKS
100–125 G (3–4 OZ) SUGAR
150–300 ML ($\frac{1}{4}$–$\frac{1}{2}$ PINT) WHIPPING OR DOUBLE CREAM (SEE ABOVE)

Scald the single cream or milk, then remove from the heat and add the chocolate and coffee. Leave to melt, then stir until smooth.

Whisk the yolks with the sugar until pale and thick, then slowly whisk in the chocolate milk.

Return to the saucepan and stir over a gentle heat until the mixture thickens. Remove from the heat and leave to cool.

Whip the cream until thick but light and fold into the cooled custard.

Pour into a freezing tray or serving dish and freeze.

Remove from the freezer half an hour before serving and keep in the refrigerator.

VARIATION: To make CHOCOLATE PRALINE ICE CREAM use a little less sugar and stir in 125–175 g (4–6 oz) praline (see page 20) before folding in the whipped cream.

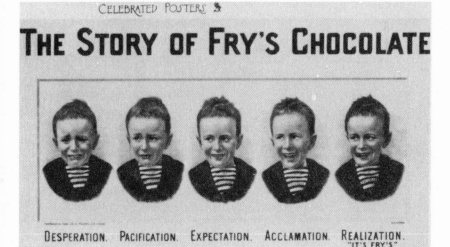

CHOCOLATE HONEYCOMB ICE

Very light, with an interesting honeycomb texture; children love this ice.

300 ML (½ PINT) SINGLE CREAM OR MILK, OR A BLEND OF
    THE TWO
125 G (4 OZ) PLAIN OR BITTER CHOCOLATE
4 EGG YOLKS
75 G (3 OZ) SUGAR
150 ML (¼ PINT) DOUBLE CREAM
2 EGG WHITES

Scald the cream or milk, then remove from the heat and add the chocolate. Leave to melt, then stir until smooth.

Meanwhile separate the eggs and whisk the yolks with the sugar until they are pale and thick, then slowly whisk in the chocolate milk.

Return to the saucepan and stir over a gentle heat until the mixture thickens. Remove from the heat and leave to cool.

Whip the cream until light and then fold in the cooled custard.

Whisk the whites until they stand in firm peaks and fold into the mixture.

Pour into a serving dish and freeze. The mixture will slightly separate and the frozen ice will have a dense texture at the bottom, and a lighter, 'honeycomb' texture on top.

Remove from the freezer half an hour before serving and leave in the refrigerator.

CHOCOLATE, MOCHA AND MARSHMALLOW ICE CREAM

1 (140 G, 5 OZ) PACKET MARSHMALLOWS
225 G (8 OZ) PLAIN OR BITTER CHOCOLATE
4 TABLESPOONS VERY STRONG COFFEE
4 EGG YOLKS
300 ML (½ PINT) DOUBLE CREAM

Melt the marshmallows, chocolate and coffee together in a basin over a pan of simmering water.

Beat the yolks until pale and fluffy, then add to the chocolate mixture slowly, stirring well. Continue to cook over simmering water until the mixture thickens slightly. Remove from the heat and leave to cool.

Whip the cream lightly and fold in. Pour into a serving dish and freeze.

NOTE: You can also keep aside a little of the chocolate, grate it coarsely, and stir it into the cooled mixture when you fold in the whipped cream.

CHOCOLATE CHESTNUT
ICE CREAM

Very rich!

3 EGG YOLKS
225 G (8 OZ) SUGAR
300 ML (½ PINT) SINGLE CREAM OR MILK
225 G (½ LB) CANNED UNSWEETENED CHESTNUT PURÉE
100 G (3½ OZ) PLAIN OR BITTER CHOCOLATE
4 TABLESPOONS RUM, BRANDY OR ORANGE LIQUEUR
300 ML (½ PINT) DOUBLE CREAM, LIGHTLY BEATEN

Beat the yolks with the sugar until they are thoroughly mixed.

Scald the single cream or milk.

Put the chestnut purée into a small bowl and add enough of the hot cream or milk to form a smooth thin paste.

Add the chocolate to the remaining cream or milk and leave until melted. Stir till smooth, then pour slowly over the yolks, beating well. Add the chestnut purée.

Place the bowl over a pan of simmering water and stir or gently beat the mixture until it begins to thicken, then leave to cool.

When quite cool add the rum, brandy or liqueur, and fold in the lightly beaten double cream.

Pour into a serving dish or into a loaf tin lined with foil and freeze.

Turn out of the tin on to a dish before serving.

CHOCOLATE PARFAIT

Velvety smooth, richly chocolaty but refreshing, this really perfect dessert is quick and easy to make provided you have a powerful electric mixer. Use unsweetened chocolate if possible; if not, be sure to add the coffee to counteract the extra sweetness, as the frozen consistency would not be as good if you used less sugar.

125 G (4 OZ) SUGAR
150 ML (¼ PINT) WATER
125 G (4 OZ) UNSWEETENED OR BITTER CHOCOLATE
4 EGG YOLKS
1 TABLESPOON BRANDY (OPTIONAL)
1 TABLESPOON VERY STRONG BLACK COFFEE (OPTIONAL)
     SEE ABOVE
300 ML (½ PINT) WHIPPING CREAM

Bring the sugar and water to the boil in a heavy saucepan, stirring until the sugar has dissolved. Boil briskly for 3 minutes. Then remove from the heat and add the chocolate, stirring until the chocolate has melted and the syrup is smooth.

Meanwhile whisk the yolks until they are pale. Slowly pour in the hot chocolate syrup and continue to whisk until the mixture has cooled. Add the brandy and coffee.

Whip the cream until light and bulky but not stiff, and fold into the cooled chocolate cream.

Pour into individual parfait glasses or ramekin dishes and freeze.

Serve straight from the freezer.

ICED CHOCOLATE SOUFFLÉ

This is the counterpart to the previous recipe – not quite as rich or dense as the Chocolate Parfait, but very light and smooth. Use unsweetened chocolate if possible, otherwise use the bitterest chocolate you can and a little less sugar. An electric beater with a balloon whisk is really essential for this recipe.

225 G (8 OZ) SUGAR
150 ML ($\frac{1}{4}$ PINT) WATER
100 G ($3\frac{1}{2}$ OZ) UNSWEETENED CHOCOLATE (SEE ABOVE)
1 TABLESPOON INSTANT COFFEE POWDER
4 EGG WHITES
300 ML ($\frac{1}{2}$ PINT) WHIPPING CREAM
For serving (optional)
2 TABLESPOONS TIA MARIA OR CRÈME DE CACAO
150 ML ($\frac{1}{4}$ PINT) WHIPPING CREAM

Bring the sugar and water slowly to the boil, stirring until the sugar has completely dissolved. Boil briskly for 3 minutes. Remove from the heat, allow to cool a little, then add the chocolate and coffee and stir until smooth.

Meanwhile whisk the egg whites until they stand in stiff peaks. As soon as the syrup is ready, pour it in a thin stream on the whites, still whisking at top speed.

Whip the cream until thick and bulky and fold it into the mixture. Pour into a freezerproof serving dish or into individual ramekin dishes and freeze.

Serve straight from the freezer with a little liqueur poured over, and topped with lightly whipped cream if you wish.

Drink Cadbury's Cocoa

"STRENGTH AND STAYING POWER."—TO ATHLETES.—*The popular beverage for Breakfast, Luncheon, Tea, and Supper, in all seasons, is CADBURY'S COCOA; a pure refined Cocoa—exhilarating, comforting, and sustaining—providing, in a concentrated form, admirable nutritive flesh-forming qualities, strength, and staying power. Cadbury's Cocoa is GUARANTEED PURE AND SOLUBLE, and the public are cautioned to see that they get the genuine article. In the whole process of manufacture the automatic machinery employed obviates the necessity of its being once touched by human hand. A 6d. Packet is sufficient for 14 large Breakfast Cups of strong delicious Cocoa. Makers to Her Majesty.*

CHOCOLATE PEPPERMINT PARFAIT

A really quick and simple recipe that is always popular. Use thin chocolate peppermint creams or wafers for best results.

25 G (I OZ) SUGAR
150 ML (¼ PINT) WATER
175 G (6 OZ) CHOCOLATE PEPPERMINT CREAMS
3 EGG YOLKS
150 ML (¼ PINT) DOUBLE CREAM
I TABLESPOON CRÈME DE MENTHE OR CHOCOLATE
PEPPERMINT LIQUEUR (OPTIONAL)

Boil the sugar and water together in a heavy saucepan for 3 minutes. Pour into a blender glass, add the chocolate peppermint creams and blend until smooth. Add the egg yolks and blend again. Leave in the blender glass to cool, and when quite cold, blend in the cream and liqueur (if using).

Pour into a bowl or individual ramekin dishes and freeze. Serve straight from the freezer.

CHOCOLATE BOMBE

A *bombe* is the most magnificent of all the ice cream confections, consisting of layers of different-flavoured ice cream surrounding the central core of meltingly light mousse, the whole frozen – ideally – in a tall, elaborately crenellated *bombe* or jelly mould and turned out just before serving.

The possibilities are endless. You can have one layer of ice cream or several, or you can start with a layer of ice cream followed by one of water ice before you get to the mousse, and you can combine any number of flavours. The central mousse can be plain or flavoured, and for a *bombe surprise*, you can hide a few liqueur chocolates in the mousse.

Coffee ice cream with chocolate bombe mousse, or chocolate ice cream (pages 123–4), with nut, praline, coffee or liqueur-flavoured mousse – especially one flavoured with a chocolate liqueur – are obvious suggestions; less obvious, but startlingly good, is a combination of raspberry water ice, or ice cream, with chocolate mousse, pineapple water ice with chocolate mousse, chocolate ice cream with whisky or crème-de-menthe-flavoured mousse, chocolate chestnut ice cream with orange-liqueur-flavoured mousse – there is no end to the scope for your imagination.

600 ML (1 PINT) ICE CREAM (SEE ABOVE)
For the mousse
75 G (3 OZ) SUGAR
4 TABLESPOONS WATER
3 EGG YOLKS

2 TABLESPOONS LIQUID FLAVOURING (OPTIONAL)
25 G (1 OZ) PLAIN OR BITTER CHOCOLATE (OPTIONAL)
150 ML ($\frac{1}{4}$ PINT) DOUBLE OR WHIPPING CREAM
2 TABLESPOONS PRALINE (SEE PAGE 20), CHOPPED NUTS,
   GLACÉ FRUIT OR MARRONS GLACÉS (OPTIONAL)
1 EGG WHITE

Chill a 1-litre (2-pint) capacity *bombe* mould or stainless steel basin and leave the ice cream at room temperature for half an hour, then press it round the sides of the mould, using a silver or metal spoon to smooth it from the bottom upwards against the sides, until the mould is completely lined with an even layer. Leave in the freezer until you have made the mousse.

Boil the sugar and water until it reaches a temperature of about 105°C (220°F) or until it forms a thick syrup. Remove from the heat.

Whisk the yolks until they are pale and fluffy, then pour on the hot syrup in a thin stream, whisking all the time. Continue to whisk at maximum speed until the mixture is quite cool.

Whisk in liquid flavouring and/or melted chocolate (see page 13).

Whip the cream lightly and fold in, together with any nuts or fruit.

Whisk the egg white until it stands in soft peaks and fold in also, then pour the mixture into the centre of the *bombe* mould and freeze. Do not keep for more than a week; the mousse loses its light texture.

"Strength and Staying Power."
CADBURY'S
COCOA
IS ABSOLUTELY PURE
CADBURY'S COCOA
SUSTAINS AGAINST FATIGUE.
INCREASES MUSCULAR STRENGTH.
GIVES PHYSICAL ENDURANCE AND STAYING POWER.
CADBURY'S ABSOLUTELY PURE COCOA is a refined concentration of the strength-sustaining and flesh-forming constituents of the Cocoa Nib. Delicious, nutritious, easily digested, and of great economy, a Sixpenny Packet yielding fourteen large breakfast cups of perfect Cocoa.

CHOCOLATE SAUCES

There are those for whom no ice cream is complete without its chocolate sauce, preferably poured over while hot, thickly congealing as it meets, and melts, the ice cream.

QUICK CHOCOLATE SAUCE

Economical and very good hot or cold. It thickens as it cools.

    175 G (6 OZ) SUGAR
    300 ML (½ PINT) WATER
    50 G (2 OZ) COCOA POWDER
    PINCH OF GROUND CINNAMON

Put all the ingredients into a saucepan and stir over low heat until the sugar has completely dissolved and the sauce is smooth. Bring quickly to the boil and boil for 1 minute.

RICH CHOCOLATE SAUCE

    225 G (8 OZ) PLAIN OR BITTER CHOCOLATE
    1 TABLESPOON VERY STRONG BLACK COFFEE
    1 TABLESPOON BRANDY
    300 ML (½ PINT) DOUBLE OR SINGLE CREAM

Put all the ingredients into a saucepan and stir over a moderate heat until the chocolate has melted and the sauce is smooth. Serve hot or cold.

BITTERSWEET CHOCOLATE SAUCE

125 G (4 OZ) PLAIN OR BITTER CHOCOLATE
175 G (6 OZ) SUGAR
300 ML (½ PINT) SINGLE OR DOUBLE CREAM
I TABLESPOON STRONG BLACK COFFEE
I TABLESPOON RUM OR BRANDY (OPTIONAL)

Put the chocolate and sugar into the top of a double boiler, or into a very heavy saucepan, and stir over gentle heat until the chocolate has melted. Cover and simmer for 20 minutes (do not allow to burn) – this gives the sauce its distinctive slightly bitter taste.

Take off the heat, stir in the cream and other ingredients and stir until smooth.

Serve hot or cold.

HOT CHOCOLATE FUDGE SAUCE

150 ML (¼ PINT) DOUBLE CREAM
50 G (2 OZ) BUTTER
50 G (2 OZ) SOFT DARK BROWN SUGAR
50 G (2 OZ) LIGHT BROWN SUGAR
25 G (I OZ) COCOA POWDER
PINCH OF SALT

Heat the cream with the butter and stir until smooth. Add both the sugars and stir over moderate heat until the sugar has dissolved and the sauce is quite smooth.

Add the cocoa and salt, stir until smooth, bring just to the boil and serve very hot.

NOTE: The sauces given earlier with Profiteroles and Pears Belle Hélène are also excellent served with ice cream.

Saml. Bennett Esqr. London Novr. 13. 1765

Bought of Richard Haines

Chocolate-Maker, at Tom's Coffee-House.

in Russell Street, Covent Garden —

WHO SELLS

Superfine Vanelloe & Plain Carracca Chocolate. Finest
Teas of all sorts, Best High Roasted Turkey Coffee.
Spanish, Havannah &c. Snuffs, Wholesale and Retail.
—— at Reasonable Rates. ——

1 lb. Supfine High Roasted Turkey Coffee — L. 7. —

Recd at the same time the Contents and all
Demands for my Father Richd. Haines

L — 7 —

Tho. Haines

CHOCOLATE COMES TO ENGLAND – AND RETURNS TO AMERICA

When Thomas Gage was on his travels in South America in the mid seventeenth century, he was shocked to see that neither the English nor the Dutch had learned to appreciate the value of cocoa: 'when we have taken a good prize, a ship laden with cacao, in anger and wrath we have hurled overboard this good commodity, not regarding the worth and goodness of it, but calling it in bad Spain *cagarruta de carnero*, or sheep dung in good English.'

The first printed reference to chocolate in England comes in 1657, when an advertisement appeared in the *Public Advertiser*:

In Bishopsgate St, in Queen's Head Alley, at a Frenchman's house, is an excellent West India drink called Chocolate to be sold, where you may have it ready at any time, and also unmade at reasonable rates.

In 1662 Henry Stubbs, newly returned from practising as a doctor in Jamaica, wrote an entire book on the subject of chocolate, entitled *The Indian Nectar, a Discourse Concerning Chocolate*. He says in his preface that chocolate has 'found the King's approbation', and recommends 'an honest though poor man, Richard Mortimer in Sun-Alley in East-Smith-Field for the purchasing of chocolate'. He also mentions

Captain Beckford's at the Customhouse Key, where 'the best chocolate, called Chocolate-Royal' can be got for 6s 6d per pound. Ordinary varieties cost 3s 8d per pound.

To the coffee houses which had been flourishing for some while were now added chocolate houses, White's and The Cocoa Tree being the most famous among them. When Samuel Pepys got horribly drunk on Charles II's Coronation Day, 23 April 1661, he records in his diary the next day:

> Waked in the morning with my head in a sad taking through last night's drink, which I am very sorry for. So rise and went out with Mr. Creed to drink our morning draught, which he did give me in chocolate to settle my stomach.

The arrival of chocolate did nothing to improve the tone of the coffee houses; and Roger North (later to become Attorney-General to James II) inveighs against them:

> The use of coffee-houses seems much improved by a new invention, called chocolate-houses, for the benefit of rooks and cullies of quality, where gaming is added to all the rest, and the summons of W— seldom fails; as if the devil had erected a new university, and those were the colleges of its professors, as well as his schools of discipline.

On 29 December 1675, Charles II issued a Proclamation for the Suppression of Coffee-Houses, which included all establishments serving chocolate, sherbet and tea, as well as coffee. But it proved completely unenforceable, and was forgotten in a matter of days.

White's became the first of the gentlemen's clubs – rather in self-defence, for the *hoi polloi* used the downstairs room for gaming:

Dissipated and broken captains, sharpers, and even highwaymen of the more presentable type were constantly to be met at the Chocolate House; judges there were liable to meet the man whom they might afterwards have to sentence in the dock; it was no uncommon thing in those days to recognize a body swinging in chains on a heath outside London as a man with whom you had called a main at hazard a few weeks before at White's or at the Cocoa Tree. So the Ministers and great lawyers and men of fashion of Queen Anne's reign very naturally retired to their own rooms at the Chocolate House, where they could lose fortunes to each other in all privacy and decorum. (From *Amusements of London*, Boulton, Vol. 1, 1901.)

This scene of gambling, dissolution and despair from Hogarth's 'Rake's Progress' takes place in White's Chocolate House

Both chocolate houses were popular meeting places until well into the eighteenth century, frequently mentioned in plays and poems of the period. Writers like Addison and Steele, and later Gibbon, were often to be seen at them and news was not only read and rumoured, but also written there: in the first number of *The Tatler*, on 12 April 1709, Steele announced that 'all accounts of gallantry, pleasure and entertainment shall be under the article of White's Chocolate House'.

In Queen Anne's reign The Cocoa Tree became known as a political house frequented by the Tories, and during the rebellion of 1745 it was regarded as the headquarters of the Jacobites.

Chocolate proved a useful source of revenue. In 1724,

Outside White's Chocolate House, from an engraving, 'The British Patriots' Procession through London', 1750

George I issued an act imposing a fine of 20 shillings for every pound of chocolate which did not bear the stamp showing that duty had been paid, and restricting the private use of chocolate.

The year 1728 saw the opening of the first English factory, in Bristol, for processing the cocoa bean, using a water engine invented by Walter Churchman. Thirty-three years later this factory was bought by Joseph Fry. Meanwhile, because of the excise duty levied, chocolate remained expensive to buy at 10–15 shillings a pound.

The eighteenth century saw one significant breakthrough in the use of chocolate. Sir Hans Sloane (of Square fame), personal physician to Samuel Pepys and Queen Anne, President of the Royal Society and virtual founder of the British Museum, had accompanied the Duke of Albemarle to Jamaica, where he became interested in the nutritional and medicinal properties of chocolate. He is credited with the inspired notion of using milk, instead of water, to make it. Sir Hans first kept his recipe a secret, but later sold it to a London apothecary, and much later it came into the possession of the Cadbury brothers.

Meanwhile in 1765 John Hannon, an Irish immigrant, arrived in America and persuaded a Dr James Baker to finance the setting-up of a chocolate factory, the first in the USA. Twelve years later, John Hannon was lost at sea on his way to the West Indies to purchase cocoa beans; Dr Baker took over the business – and an American institution was born.

All this while, however, the drink made from the cocoa bean remained heavy and fatty, and needed additives to make it palatable. For the discovery of how the fats could be extracted, we must wait until the nineteenth century.

Chocolate Is Good For You

Chocolate is not only pleasant to taste, but it is a veritable balm of the mouth, for the maintaining of all glands and humours in a good state of health. Thus it is that all who drink it, possess a sweet breath.

Dr S. Blancardi, Amsterdam 1705

There died recently in Martinique a Councillor of about 100 years of age, who subsisted for thirty years on nothing other than chocolate and some biscuits. Occasionally he would take a little soup to eat, but at no time meat, fish or other nourishment. Yet he was so fit that, at the age of eighty-five years, he could still mount his horse without stirrups.

From the chronicles of a Dutch traveller, c. 1720

Alexander von Humboldt, the great nineteenth-century German traveller in South America, writes of cocoa as a natural phenomenon: 'on no other occasion apart from this specific instance, has nature concentrated in so small a space such an abundance of the most valuable nourishment'.

If any man has drunk a little too deeply from the cup of physical pleasure; if he has spent too much time at his desk that should have been spent asleep; if his fine spirits have temporarily become dulled; if he finds the air too damp, the minutes too slow, and the atmosphere too heavy to withstand; if he is obsessed by a fixed idea which bars him from any freedom of thought: if he is any of these poor creatures, we say, let him be given a good pint of amber-flavored chocolate, in the proportions of sixty to seventy-two grains of amber to a pound, and marvels will be performed.

J.-A. Brillat-Savarin, *Physiologie du goût*, 1825

And modern science tells us that chocolate is a quick-energy food, which contains protein, fat, carbohydrate, calcium, phosphorus, iron, sodium, potassium, vitamin A, thiamine, riboflavin and niacin.

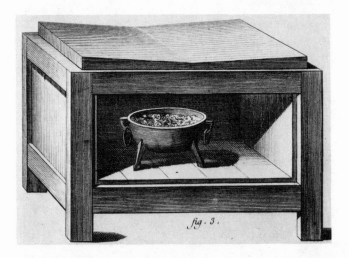

An eighteenth-century crushing board for cocoa beans from Diderot and d'Alembert, *Encyclopédie*

CHAPTER
5

CAKES

CADBURY'S COCOA

"The typical Cocoa of English Manufacture — Absolutely Pure."
—*The Analyst.*

CADBURY'S COCOA is closely allied to milk in the large proportion of flesh-forming and strength sustaining elements that it contains. It is prepared on the principle of excluding the superabundance of fatty indigestible matter with which Cocoa abounds—supplying a refined thin infusion of absolutely pure Cocoa, exhilarating and refreshing for Breakfast, Luncheon, Tea, or Supper—giving staying power, and imparting new life and vigour to growing Children, and those of delicate constitutions.

A Small Spoonful of Cadbury's Cocoa, with boiling water or milk, will make a large Breakfast Cup of the most delicious, digestible, absolutely pure and nourishing Cocoa, of the greatest strength and the finest flavour, entirely free from any admixture.

CADBURY'S COCOA IS THE BEST BEVERAGE FOR CHILDREN.

QUICK CHOCOLATE CAKE

Almost instant, economical and very basic, this is one of those 'never fail' family recipes that everyone should have in their repertoire. To be truly quick, you need an electric mixer, and should use a soft margarine.

125 G (4 OZ) SELF-RAISING FLOUR
I TEASPOON BAKING POWDER
125 G (4 OZ) CASTER SUGAR
125 G (4 OZ) SOFT MARGARINE
2 LARGE OR 3 SMALL EGGS
25 G (I OZ) COCOA POWDER
I TEASPOON INSTANT COFFEE POWDER
3 TABLESPOONS VERY HOT WATER

For the icing
100 G (4 OZ) ICING SUGAR
25 G (I OZ) COCOA POWDER
50 G (2 OZ) BUTTER
3 TABLESPOONS WATER
75 G (3 OZ) SUGAR

Set the oven at gas mark 4 (180°C) 350°F.

Sift the flour and baking powder into a large mixing bowl, add sugar, margarine and eggs. Mix the cocoa and coffee powder to a smooth paste with water just off the boil and add to the bowl.

Starting on the lowest speed, begin to mix the ingredients, and as soon as they begin to blend increase the speed and beat at top speed for one minute only.

Divide the mixture between two buttered or non-stick 18 or 20 cm (7–8 in) diameter sandwich tins, spreading the mixture evenly and smoothing the top, and bake for 25–30 minutes, until the tops of the cakes are firm. Turn out on to wire trays and leave to cool.

Sift the icing sugar and cocoa into a bowl.

Put the remaining ingredients into a small saucepan and heat gently, stirring till the sugar is dissolved. Bring to the boil and immediately pour into the bowl, stirring to a smooth, thin cream.

Leave to cool until the cake is ready to be iced: the mixture will thicken as it cools.

When the cake has cooled, use half the mixture to sandwich the two cakes together and spread remaining icing over the top.

*   *   *   *   *   *   *   *   *

*   Katharine Hepburn, seventy, actress, asked how   *
     she stays trim: 'I don't have to watch my figure as
     I never had much of one to watch. What you see
*   before you is the result of a lifetime of chocolate.'   *

*   *Time Magazine*, 17 November 1980   *

*   *   *   *   *   *   *   *   *

MARBLE CAKE

An old-time children's favourite.

175 G (6 OZ) BUTTER OR MARGARINE
175 G (6 OZ) SUGAR
3 LARGE EGGS
175 G (6 OZ) FLOUR
1 TEASPOON BAKING POWDER
GRATED RIND OF ½ LEMON
1 TABLESPOON COCOA POWDER
1 TABLESPOON ICING SUGAR

Set the oven at gas mark 4 (180°C) 350°F.

Generously butter a 20 cm (8 in) diameter kugelhopf tin or use a springform baking tin with the central funnel, and sprinkle with fine breadcrumbs or ground almonds.

Cream the butter with the sugar until very light and fluffy, then add the eggs one by one and continue to beat until the mixture is very light.

Sift the flour with the baking powder and fold in.

Divide the mixture into almost equal halves and add the grated lemon rind to the larger 'half'.

Blend the cocoa thoroughly into the remaining part of the mixture.

Spoon half the white mixture into the bottom of the cake tin. Top with half the chocolate mixture and repeat. The layers will be uneven, and give a 'marbled' effect after baking. Smooth over the top and bake for 50 minutes to 1 hour, or until a skewer inserted into the centre of the cake comes out clean.

Leave to cool a little, then turn out of the tin on to a wire baking tray, and when almost cooled, sprinkle the top with the sifted icing sugar.

RICH CHOCOLATE CAKE

This is a really rich, dark cake – the kind indulgent mothers might put into a school tuck box as it keeps moist for a long time.

225 G (8 OZ) BUTTER OR MARGARINE
225 G (8 OZ) SUGAR
1 TABLESPOON VERY STRONG BLACK COFFEE
1 TABLESPOON SHERRY
4 EGGS
100 G (3½ OZ) COCOA POWDER
225 G (8 OZ) SELF-RAISING FLOUR
125 G (4 OZ) GROUND ALMONDS

For the butter icing
100 G (3½ OZ) PLAIN OR BITTER CHOCOLATE
1 TABLESPOON VERY STRONG BLACK COFFEE
75 G (3 OZ) UNSALTED BUTTER
150 G (5 OZ) ICING SUGAR
1 TABLESPOON SHERRY (OPTIONAL)

For the glacé icing
100 G (3½ OZ) PLAIN OR BITTER CHOCOLATE
2 TABLESPOONS WATER
75 G (3 OZ) ICING SUGAR
15 G (½ OZ) BUTTER

Set the oven at gas mark 4 (180°C) 350°F.

Cream the butter or margarine and sugar together until white and very fluffy.

Beat in the coffee and sherry.

Beat the eggs together lightly with a fork.

Sift the cocoa and flour together, and blend in the ground almonds.

Alternately beat the eggs and the dry ingredients into the butter mixture.

Pour into a well-greased 25 cm (10 in) diameter baking tin, preferably a springform tin, and bake for about 1 hour, or until the top has risen slightly and is firm to the touch, and a skewer inserted into the centre of the cake comes out clean.

Allow to cool for about 15 minutes, then remove from the tin and leave to cool thoroughly on a wire cake rack.

To make the butter icing, melt the chocolate with the coffee (see page 13). Stir until smooth and leave to cool a little.

Beat the butter and sugar together until very light and fluffy. Beat in the chocolate and the sherry.

When the cake is quite cold, split it across the centre and sandwich together with the butter icing.

Make the chocolate glacé icing by putting the chocolate into a small saucepan with the water. Stir over a low heat until the chocolate has melted and forms a smooth sauce. Add the icing sugar, stir until smooth, then raise the heat and bring to the boil. Boil, stirring constantly, until a small amount of the mixture dropped into cold water forms a soft ball (116°C or 240°F on a sugar thermometer), and the mixture in the pan begins to throw thick bubbles. Remove from the heat, stir in the butter and pour quickly and evenly over the cake, smoothing any surplus that drips off round the sides of the cake.

Leave to set for at least 1 hour before serving.

TRUFFLE CAKE

A bitter-sweet, intensely chocolaty cake, with just a hint of
orange, filled and covered with a rich truffle mixture – how
much more satisfyingly chocolaty can·you get?

For the cake
200 G (7 OZ) PLAIN OR BITTER CHOCOLATE
100 G (4 OZ) UNSALTED BUTTER
2 TABLESPOONS CASTER SUGAR
4 EGGS
75 G (3 OZ) FLOUR
½ TEASPOON BAKING POWDER
ICING SUGAR, FOR DUSTING (OPTIONAL)

For the filling
225 G (8 OZ) PLAIN OR BITTER CHOCOLATE
225 G (8 OZ) UNSALTED BUTTER
225 G (8 OZ) ICING SUGAR
4 TABLESPOONS ORANGE JUICE
4 TABLESPOONS ORANGE CURAÇAO

Set the oven at gas mark 4 (180°C) 350°F.

Melt the chocolate (see page 13), stir till smooth and leave
to cool.

Beat the butter with 1 tablespoon of caster sugar until pale
and fluffy. Separate the eggs and beat in the yolks one by one.
Beat in the melted, cooled chocolate.

Sift the flour with the baking powder and fold into the
mixture.

Beat the whites until they begin to stand in peaks, then beat
in the remaining caster sugar. Fold the cake mixture gently

but thoroughly into the meringue. Pour into a buttered 20 cm (8 in) diameter cake tin, preferably springform or loose-bottomed, and bake for 40–45 minutes, or until a skewer inserted just comes out clean. Remove from the oven, leave to cool a little, then turn out of the tin and leave to cool on a wire rack.

Prepare the filling as for making Quick Truffles (page 279), and beat in half the orange juice and liqueur.

When the cake is quite cold, slice it in half and lightly dribble the remaining orange juice and liqueur over both halves.

Sandwich the cake together with half the truffle mixture and spread or pipe the remainder over the top.

Lightly dust with a little icing sugar before serving, if you wish.

CHOCOLATE SPONGE CAKE

Very light, and best eaten very fresh, sandwiched with vanilla-flavoured, lightly whipped cream. You can also flavour the cream with puréed, sieved raspberries, as these blend particularly well with chocolate.

3 LARGE EGGS
PINCH OF SALT
125 G (4 OZ) SUGAR
75 G (3 OZ) FLOUR
½ TEASPOON BAKING POWDER
20 G (¾ OZ) COCOA POWDER

For the filling
300 ML (½ PINT) DOUBLE OR WHIPPING CREAM
A FEW DROPS VANILLA ESSENCE
ICING SUGAR, FOR DREDGING

Set the oven at gas mark 6 (200°C) 400°F.

Separate the eggs and whisk the whites with the pinch of salt until they stand in peaks. Slowly whisk in the sugar. Beat the yolks together lightly with a fork and whisk them into the whites very slowly. In this way the mixture should remain very thick, light and bulky.

Sift the flour together with the baking powder and the cocoa, and fold lightly but thoroughly into the sponge mixture, using a tablespoon or a spatula.

Butter two 20 or 23 cm (8 or 9 in) diameter sandwich tins and dredge them lightly with flour. Divide the mixture evenly between the two tins, smooth over the tops and bake for 25 minutes, or until the tops have risen but are firm, and the cake has shrunk a little from the sides.

Leave to cool for 5 minutes, then turn out on to a wire cake rack.

Whip the cream lightly with the vanilla essence and a teaspoon of icing sugar, and sandwich the cakes together when cool. Dust the top with a little more icing sugar.

GÂTEAU MONT BLANC

A quick and easy dessert cake.

200 G (7 OZ) PLAIN OR BITTER CHOCOLATE
40 G (1½ OZ) BUTTER
3 EGGS
75 G (3 OZ) SUGAR
50 G (2 OZ) SELF-RAISING FLOUR
½ TEASPOON BAKING POWDER
I TABLESPOON RUM
300 ML (½ PINT) WHIPPING CREAM

Set the oven at gas mark 5 (190°C) 375°F.

Melt the chocolate (see page 13), remove from the heat and add the butter. Stir until smooth.

Separate the eggs and whisk the yolks with the sugar until pale and fluffy. Beat in the chocolate butter mixture.

Sift the flour with the baking powder and blend into the mixture. Add the rum.

Whisk the egg whites until they stand in soft peaks. Fold into the mixture.

Pour into a buttered kugelhopf or ring mould and bake in the centre of the oven for 30 minutes, or until a skewer inserted into the centre just comes out clean.

Leave to cool then remove from the tin on to a serving dish.

Lightly whip the cream and pile into the centre of the cake, allowing it to flow down the sides to give a snowy mountain effect.

CHOCOLATE, ALMOND AND RUM CAKE

More dessert than cake, this is extremely rich and should be soft and fudgy in the centre. Eat with a spoon or fork, and cover with whipped cream if you like.
It is just as good made with hazelnuts instead of almonds.

125 G (4 OZ) PLAIN OR BITTER CHOCOLATE
2–3 DROPS ALMOND ESSENCE (OMIT IF USING HAZELNUTS)
2 TABLESPOONS RUM
125 G (4 OZ) UNSALTED BUTTER
125 G (4 OZ) CASTER SUGAR
3 LARGE EGGS
50 G (2 OZ) BLANCHED ALMONDS, FINELY GROUND
PINCH OF SALT
2 TABLESPOONS FLOUR

Set the oven at gas mark 4 (180°C) 350°F.

Melt the chocolate with the almond essence and the rum (see page 13). Stir until quite smooth, then leave to cool.

Meanwhile, beat the butter and all but 1 tablespoon of the sugar together until they are quite white and fluffy, then beat in the egg yolks one by one.

Combine the butter and chocolate mixtures and stir until they are really well blended. Stir in the ground almonds.

Whisk the egg whites with the pinch of salt until they begin to stand in peaks, then sprinkle in the extra tablespoon of caster sugar and continue to whisk until they stand in very firm peaks.

Stir in a quarter of the egg whites to lighten the mixture. Add half the remaining egg whites to the bowl, sift on half the flour and, using a spatula, cut and fold into the mixture until well amalgamated. Repeat with remaining egg whites and flour. Fold very lightly, but make sure that no patches of white remain.

Pour the mixture into a buttered and floured 23 cm (9 in) diameter sandwich tin and cook in the centre of the oven for 30–35 minutes, until there is a pale crust on top, the sides of the cake are set, and a skewer inserted near the edge comes out clean, but the centre is still quite soft.

Remove from the oven, allow to cool for 10 minutes, then turn out on to a cake rack and leave to cool completely.

Serve plain or topped with whipped cream.

CHOCOLATE AND FRUIT
TEABREAD

Light, dry and very pleasant, with just a hint of spice.

50 G (2 OZ) PLAIN OR BITTER CHOCOLATE
50 G (2 OZ) MIXED CANDIED PEEL
50 G (2 OZ) BLANCHED ALMONDS
125 G (4 OZ) BUTTER OR MARGARINE
75 G (3 OZ) SOFT LIGHT BROWN SUGAR
75 G (3 OZ) GRANULATED SUGAR
3 EGGS
175 G (6 OZ) FLOUR
½ TEASPOON BAKING POWDER
½ TEASPOON GROUND CINNAMON
PINCH GRATED NUTMEG
PINCH GROUND CLOVES
2 TABLESPOONS MILK OR SOURED MILK
PINCH OF SALT

Set the oven at gas mark 4 (180°C) 350°F.

Melt the chocolate (see page 13) and leave to cool.

Chop the candied peel and the almonds fairly finely.

Cream the butter or margarine with both sugars until very fluffy. Separate the eggs, add the yolks one by one and continue to beat until the mixture is very light. Beat in the chocolate.

Sift the flour with the baking powder and the spices and blend into the mixture alternately with the milk.

Fold in the peel and the nuts.

Whisk the egg whites with the pinch of salt until they

stand in peaks but are not dry. Fold carefully but thoroughly into the mixture.

Pour into a buttered 10 × 30 cm (4 × 12 in) loaf tin, and bake for 45–50 minutes, or until a skewer inserted into the cake comes out clean.

Remove from the oven and leave to cool a little before turning out on to a wire rack.

Allow to cool before serving.

CHOCOLATE NUT LOAF

A delicious tea or breakfast bread.

15 G (½ OZ) FRESH YEAST
60 G (2 OZ) SUGAR
75 ML (⅛ PINT) MILK
250 G (9 OZ) FLOUR
PINCH OF SALT
75 G (3 OZ) BUTTER
1 EGG

For the filling
125 G (4 OZ) HAZELNUTS
3 TABLESPOONS COCOA POWDER
3 TABLESPOONS MILK
175 G (6 OZ) SUGAR
3–4 PLAIN OR PLAIN CHOCOLATE DIGESTIVE BISCUITS
1 EGG

To finish
MELTED BUTTER
ICING SUGAR

Cream the yeast with 1 teaspoon of the sugar and a little of the warmed milk and leave in a warm place until it begins to froth.

Meanwhile sift the flour and salt into a bowl, sprinkle on the remaining sugar and make a well in the centre.

Add the butter to the remaining milk and leave over a gentle heat until the butter has melted.

Pour the frothing yeast mixture into the centre of the bowl

and begin to work in some of the flour. Slowly add the milk and butter and the lightly beaten egg and work into a smooth dough.

Beat with a wooden spoon until the dough begins to throw bubbles and comes away clean from the sides of the bowl.

Cover with a clean cloth and leave in a warm place until it has risen to at least twice its bulk.

Meanwhile make the filling: roast or toast the hazelnuts until they are golden brown and the skins are loose and you can rub or blow them off (into the sink or out of doors).

Mix the cocoa to a smooth paste with the milk and stir over a low heat until it thickens.

Grate or grind the hazelnuts finely. Blend with the sugar and the biscuits crushed to a fine powder. Add the cocoa mixture and the lightly beaten egg and blend until smooth.

If you have a food processor you can put in all the ingredients together and blend till smooth.

When the dough is ready, flour a clean tea-towel lightly and roll out the dough on it to about $\frac{1}{2}$ cm ($\frac{1}{4}$ in) thick. Spread evenly with the filling, leaving a 1 cm ($\frac{1}{2}$ in) margin all around.

You can now either roll the dough up lengthwise into a Swiss roll and place in a buttered baking ring, or you can roll both sides towards the middle to form a double snail, and place in a buttered loaf tin.

Leave to rise again for at least half an hour.

Heat the oven to gas mark 5 (190°C) 375°F and bake the loaf in the centre of the oven for 45–50 minutes.

Remove from the oven when the top is firm and well risen, and leave to cool a little, then turn out of the tin on to a wire tray. Brush with melted butter and dust generously with icing sugar.

CHOCOLATE KUGELHOPF 1

A kugelhopf (or gugelhopf or kugelhupf or whichever way
you wish to spell it) is a very light yeast cake or bread, often
eaten in Germany and Austria for breakfast on Sundays and
feastdays. A chocolate version makes for an even more
sybaritic breakfast, but the icing should be thin and not too
sweet, so it is important to use unsweetened chocolate if
possible. The authentic kugelhopf is baked in a special
slantingly fluted ring mould, and the dough should rise well
above the mould during cooking, so that the cake looks like
a crown sitting on a pillow, or like a sultan's turban, which
it is also sometimes called.

10 G (SCANT ½ OZ) FRESH YEAST
125 G (4 OZ) CASTER SUGAR
275 G (10 OZ) FLOUR
75 ML (⅛ PINT) MILK
50 G (2 OZ) RAISINS (OPTIONAL)
125 G (4 OZ) CANDIED PEEL
125 G (4 OZ) BLANCHED ALMONDS
125 G (4 OZ) CHOCOLATE CHIPS (OPTIONAL)
2 TABLESPOONS RUM OR BRANDY
125 G (4 OZ) BUTTER
PINCH OF SALT
2 EGGS

For the icing
75 G (3 OZ) SUGAR
4 TABLESPOONS WATER
75 G (3 OZ) UNSWEETENED OR BITTER CHOCOLATE

Cream the yeast with a teaspoonful each of the sugar and

flour. Add the slightly warmed milk, cover and leave in a warm place till it froths.

Chop the raisins and the peel fairly coarsely, and cut the almonds into slivers. Mix with the chocolate chips, pour on the rum or brandy and leave to soak.

Melt the butter very gently and leave to cool.

When the yeast mixture is ready, sift the rest of the flour with the salt into a basin and sprinkle on the remaining sugar. Make a well in the centre and pour in the yeast, together with the butter.

Beat the eggs together lightly and pour them also into the well.

Gradually work in the flour with a wooden spoon, then knead lightly on a floured surface until the dough comes away clean from the board.

Put the dough back into the cleaned, lightly floured bowl, sprinkle with a little more flour, cover with a clean cloth and leave to rise in a warm place for at least one hour, or until the dough has doubled in bulk.

Knock down and form into a fat sausage shape. Flatten it, and sprinkle on half the fruit, nut and chocolate mixture. Fold over lengthwise, flatten out again and sprinkle on remainder. Fold over once more and fit into a buttered and floured 20 cm (8 in) diameter kugelhopf tin. The dough should come about half-way up the tin. Leave to rise again until it reaches the top of the tin.

Heat the oven to gas mark 4 (180°C) 350°F. Bake in the centre of the oven for 45 minutes, or until the cake has risen well above the top of the mould, and the top is lightly browned and springy to the touch.

Remove from the oven, leave for 10 minutes, then turn out on to a wire tray and leave to cool.

To make the icing, bring the sugar and water to the boil, stirring all the time until the sugar has dissolved. Remove from the heat, add the chocolate and stir until it has melted and the mixture is quite smooth.

Return to the heat and boil until it reaches 114°C (237°F) on a sugar thermometer, or until a small amount of the mixture, dropped into cold water, just forms a soft ball. Remove from the heat immediately and continue to stir until it stops bubbling. Pour carefully over the cake, turning it as you go so that the cake becomes completely covered. Scoop up any icing that runs down the sides and centre and smooth it back on to the cake. You must work very quickly as this icing sets very fast and loses its shine if worked with too much. If it does set too fast, add a little water and bring just to the boil again.

CHOCOLATE KUGELHOPF 2

Sweeter and a little heavier than the previous recipe, but as this version does not use yeast, it is much simpler to make. Since this, too, is really a breakfast cake, it should not be too sweet and is also best made with unsweetened chocolate. If that is unobtainable, use 25 g (1 oz) less sugar.

125 G (4 OZ) UNSWEETENED OR BITTER CHOCOLATE
200 G (7 OZ) PLAIN FLOUR
1 TEASPOON BAKING POWDER
PINCH OF SALT
¾ TEASPOON GROUND CINNAMON
¼ TEASPOON GROUND CLOVES
¼ TEASPOON ALLSPICE
125 G (4 OZ) CANDIED PEEL
50 G (2 OZ) RAISINS (OPTIONAL)
125 G (4 OZ) BLANCHED ALMONDS
2 TABLESPOONS BRANDY
3 EGGS
175 G (6 OZ) SUGAR

For the icing
2 TABLESPOONS BRANDY
6 TABLESPOONS ICING SUGAR

Set the oven at gas mark 2 (150°C) 300°F.

Butter a 20 cm (8 in) diameter kugelhopf tin and flour it lightly. Melt the chocolate (see page 13) and leave to cool. Sift the flour with the baking powder, salt and spices.

Chop the peel and raisins fairly coarsely and cut the almonds into slivers. Leave them to soak in the brandy.

Beat the eggs until they begin to froth, then beat in the sugar and continue to beat for at least 10 minutes until very light and spongy.

Beat in the cooled chocolate.

Sift the flour mixture into the mixing bowl bit by bit and fold in gently, alternating with the fruit and nut mixture.

When everything is well blended, pour into the prepared kugelhopf tin and bake for 1 hour, or until the top is firm and a skewer inserted comes out clean.

Remove from the oven, leave to cool for 10 minutes then turn out on to a wire tray.

When the cake has cooled completely, stir the brandy into the sifted icing sugar to make a smooth icing, and pour over the cake so that the top is covered and the icing runs down into the grooves of the cake. Use more icing, if you prefer to cover the cake completely.

Leave to set in a cool, dry place before serving.

FABRICATION DU CHOCOLAT. ATELIER DE BROYAGE

BAUMKUCHEN
Tree Trunk Cake

This dry biscuity cake is a German speciality. A true *Baum-kuchen* looks like a gnarled, hollow tree trunk, with brown icing on the outside. It must be sliced horizontally to reveal the inside ringed like an ancient tree. The cake is baked in layers round a central core, and this can only be properly produced by experts with the right equipment. However, this home version (which looks more like plywood) is also intriguing to look at when sliced, and it tastes delicious. It should have only the merest hint of chocolate icing.

225 G (8 OZ) UNSALTED BUTTER
225 G (8 OZ) SUGAR
225 G (8 OZ) CORNFLOUR OR
  125 G (4 OZ) CORNFLOUR AND
  100 G (4 OZ) SUPERFINE CAKE FLOUR
5 LARGE EGGS
2 TABLESPOONS BRANDY

For the icing
50 G (2 OZ) PLAIN OR BITTER CHOCOLATE
$\frac{1}{4}$ TEASPOON VEGETABLE OIL

Set the oven at gas mark 6 (200°C) 400°F.

Beat the butter and sugar together until very light and fluffy. Sift the flour and gradually beat into the mixture.

Beat in the eggs, one by one, and then the brandy.

Butter a 20 cm (8 in) diameter springform tin very generously, and spread a little of the mixture in a $\frac{1}{2}$ cm ($\frac{1}{4}$ in) thin layer on the bottom. Place near the top of the oven and bake for 10 minutes, or until it is pale brown. Spread another layer, even thinner this time if possible, evenly over the top and bake for a further 10 minutes, or until it, too, is pale brown. Continue until all the mixture has been used and the top layer is also gently browned. It is important that each layer is really light brown on top, otherwise the cake will not have the characteristic 'ringed' appearance.

Remove from the oven, allow to cool a little, then loosen the sides of the tin and leave the cake to cool further, removing the bottom of the tin after a little while and leaving the cake to cool on a wire tray.

Melt the chocolate (see page 13). Add the vegetable oil. Spread very thinly and evenly over the top and sides and leave to dry.

REHRÜCKEN
Saddle of Venison Cake

Light and slightly nutty, this much-loved German cake is baked in a special fluted and ridged mould, so that it resembles a stylized saddle of venison. Slivered, blanched almonds are inserted at regular intervals to represent the larding of the saddle. It looks beautiful, and makes an attractive and unusual birthday cake with candles placed in a straight line down the central spine. The traditional ridged cake tins, with a long central indentation to indicate the backbone of the saddle, are available in specialist kitchen shops, but the cake will taste just as delicious made in an ordinary 1 kg (2 lb) loaf tin.

50 G (2 OZ) HAZELNUTS
50 G (2 OZ) PLAIN OR BITTER CHOCOLATE
175 G (6 OZ) BUTTER
175 G (6 OZ) SUGAR
4 EGGS, SEPARATED
175 G (6 OZ) SELF-RAISING FLOUR
I TEASPOON BAKING POWDER
FINELY GRATED RIND OF ½ LEMON
PINCH OF SALT

For the icing
100 G (3½ OZ) PLAIN OR BITTER CHOCOLATE
50 G (2 OZ) ICING SUGAR
75 ML (⅛ PINT) WATER

For decoration
12 BLANCHED ALMONDS

Set the oven at gas mark 6 (200°C) 400°F.

Butter the cake tin generously and sprinkle with fine breadcrumbs or flour. Knock off any excess.

Roast or toast the hazelnuts till golden brown, then blow off the skins (out of doors or into the sink). Leave to cool then grind them finely.

Melt the chocolate (see page 13) and leave to cool.

Cream the butter with the sugar until very pale and fluffy, then beat in the egg yolks one by one, and continue to beat until the mixture is very light.

Beat in the ground hazelnuts and the melted chocolate.

Sift the flour with the baking powder and blend into the mixture together with the grated lemon rind.

Whisk the egg whites with the pinch of salt until they stand in peaks but are not dry. Fold into the mixture lightly but thoroughly, and pour into the prepared cake tin.

Bake for 45–50 minutes, leave to cool a little in the oven with the door propped open, then take out of the oven and turn out of the tin. Leave to cool on a wire tray and set the tray over a sheet of foil before icing and decorating.

To make the icing, put the chocolate, icing sugar and water into a small saucepan and stir over a moderate heat until smooth. Raise the heat and boil until the mixture reaches 114°C (237°F) on a sugar thermometer, or until a small amount dropped into cold water just forms a soft ball.

Pour the icing very quickly and evenly over the cake. With a palette knife scrape up any of the icing that drips on to the foil, and smooth it back over the cake. It is important to work fast as the icing should set quickly. Try pouring a little over the cake first − if it is too runny, it needs to be boiled a little longer. If it sets too fast, add a little water to the pan, stir until smooth and heat again.

Split the almonds and cut each half into 3 or 4 slivers lengthwise. Spike the cake evenly with these all over.

Leave the icing to set for a few hours before serving.

CADBURY'S COCOA

Absolutely Pure, therefore Best

CADBURY'S COCOA is appreciated throughout the world as a pure, delicious beverage, entirely free from adulteration. It is at once a refreshing, stimulating drink, and a nutritious food—probably more nourishing than any other beverage. It is light, refined, and digestible, and can be safely and beneficially taken as an article of daily diet AT ALL TIMES and ALL SEASONS.

CADBURY'S

IS A PURE COCOA

Made amidst Pure and Healthful Surroundings.

" The most popular of the cocoas of to-day is that made in that most pleasant of manufactories—the factory in a garden—of Cadbury Brothers, at Bournville, near Birmingham. Cadbury's name is in itself a guarantee of purity of manufacture and absolute freedom from alkaline adulteration. It represents, on the authority of the *Lancet*, the STANDARD OF HIGHEST PURITY at present attainable in regard to Cocoa."

"The typical cocoa of English manufacture—absolutely pure."
— THE ANALYST.

SACHERTORTE

The most famous of all the Viennese cakes, Sachertorte has been the subject of a great many myths, stories and arguments. This is how Joseph Wechsberg tells the tale in *The Cooking of Vienna's Empire* (Time-Life Books).

It is not true, as one legend has it, that the *Sachertorte* was invented by the notorious Frau Anna Sacher. This formidable, cigar-smoking owner of the Hotel Sacher irritated His Majesty, the ascetic Emperor Franz Joseph I, by encouraging the frivolous goings-on between the youthful archdukes and the lithe, lissom members of the Vienna Opera ballet. In fact, the *Sachertorte* had been invented in 1832 by the founder of the Sacher line, Franz, while he was serving as Prince Metternich's chef.

'He bothered me all the time to invent something new, as though my pastries were not good enough,' Franz Sacher said. 'So I just threw some ingredients together and that's it.' 'He' was Prince Metternich, and 'it' became the *Sachertorte*. Fortunately the Prince didn't demand that it be called *Metternichtorte*. He might have, if he had foreseen its world-wide success, but even a Metternich cannot foresee the future.

Since then there have been countless recipes for the 'Original' *Sachertorte*. It is the only *Torte* on earth that became the issue of a celebrated court case, which created more excitement in Vienna and consumed more newspaper space than a minor war. The issue was: who had the right to call his product the 'genuine' *Sachertorte* – the Hotel Sacher, which traded on the family connection with the *Sachertorte*'s creator, or Demel's, which had bought the right to fix the 'Genuine *Sachertorte*' seal (in the finest plain chocolate, of course) on its *Torten*? Demel's had acquired the right from Edouard Sacher, the grandson of creator Franz Sacher and the last scion of the dynasty. The recipe was published, with Edouard Sacher's permission, in *Die Wiener Konditorei*, by Hans Skrach. It starts out with 14 egg yolks, just to give you an idea of its scope.

The question kept the public and the courts of Vienna busy for seven long years. It is known in Vienna as the 'Sweet Seven Years' War'. Eventually, Austria's highest court decided that the Hotel Sacher had the right to make and sell the 'Genuine *Sachertorte*'. That was the end of the law-suit, but not of the popular argument. Demel's promptly announced they were going to sell the *Ur-Sachertorte*, the very first version. Since then a great many people, including some prominent members of the Sugar Bakers' Guild, have spoken out in favour of Demel's. Both Demel's and the Hotel Sacher send their *Sachertorten* in wooden boxes all over the world, and one can only say that both versions are light, delicate and distinctive.

Vienna's leading chefs are no help when it comes to defining the proper recipe for the *Sachertorte*. A former Demel's man puts the apricot jam inside, a method frowned upon by other experts.

While not pretending to be the 'genuine' Sachertorte, nor yet the 'Ur-Sachertorte', this recipe is as near to the Viennese taste as I can get. The cake should be very dark and chocolaty, but fairly dry, with a sweet, dark icing. I have given instructions for slicing the cake in half and sandwiching it with the apricot glaze, but those who prefer can halve the quantity of the glaze, and only brush the top thinly with it. The chocolate used should be as bitter as possible, and the bitter almond essence is an essential ingredient which makes all the difference to the final taste of the cake.

175 G (6 OZ) BITTER CHOCOLATE
125 G (4 OZ) UNSALTED BUTTER
125 G (4 OZ) SUGAR

4 EGG YOLKS
¼ TEASPOON BITTER ALMOND ESSENCE
125 G (4 OZ) FLOUR
¼ TEASPOON BAKING POWDER
5 EGG WHITES
PINCH OF SALT

For the glaze
2 TABLESPOONS APRICOT JAM
1 TABLESPOON WATER
GOOD SQUEEZE LEMON JUICE

For the icing
75 G (3 OZ) SUGAR
4 TABLESPOONS WATER
100 G (3½ OZ) BITTER CHOCOLATE

Set the oven at gas mark 3 (160°C) 325°F.

Melt the chocolate (see page 13).

Cream the butter with the sugar until very light and fluffy, then add the egg yolks one by one and continue to beat until the mixture is light and smooth. Blend in the melted chocolate and the almond essence.

Sift the flour with the baking powder and then sift again into the mixing bowl. Fold the flour into the mixture, using a metal spoon or spatula, until thoroughly blended.

Whisk the egg whites with the salt until they are stiff but not dry, and incorporate into the mixture, folding gently but thoroughly with a metal spoon or spatula, until no streaks of white remain.

Pour into a buttered and floured loose-bottomed 25 cm (10 in) diameter baking tin, and bake in the centre of the oven for 1 hour, or until the cake is firm to the touch and has shrunk slightly from the sides of the tin.

Leave to cool a little, then remove the cake from the tin and allow it to cool thoroughly on a wire rack before glazing and icing.

To make the glaze, heat the apricot jam with the water and lemon juice and bring briefly to the boil. If necessary, pass through a nylon strainer. Slice the cake in half and sandwich together with most of the glaze. Brush the remainder over the top of the cake so that it is only just moist. Leave to set.

To make the icing, bring the sugar and water to the boil, stirring all the time until the sugar has dissolved. Remove from the heat, add the chocolate and stir until the chocolate has completely melted and the mixture is quite smooth. Return to the heat and boil until a temperature of 116°C (240°F) has been reached on a sugar thermometer, or a small amount of the mixture dropped into cold water forms a soft ball.

Remove immediately from the heat, and continue to stir until the mixture ceases to bubble.

Pour quickly and evenly over the top of the cake, allowing the icing to flow down the sides. Use a palette knife to smooth the icing round the sides of the cake but do not touch the top, or it will lose its sheen.

If you like you can keep back a small part of the icing, and when the icing on the cake has begun to set, warm the remainder slightly, adding a drop of water if necessary, and drip the famous Sacher signature over the top of the cake from the tip of a spoon or knife.

DOBOSTORTE

This famous Hungarian *Torte* is a many-layered confection of light sponge cake, alternating with chocolate cream and topped with a crunchy caramel glaze.

For the cake
225 G (8 OZ) UNSALTED BUTTER
225 G (8 OZ) SUGAR
4 LARGE EGGS
175 G (6 OZ) SELF-RAISING FLOUR
¼ TEASPOON BAKING POWDER
PINCH OF SALT

For the chocolate cream
100 G (3½ OZ) PLAIN OR BITTER CHOCOLATE
175 G (6 OZ) SUGAR
75 ML (GENEROUS ⅛ PINT) WATER
175 G (6 OZ) UNSALTED BUTTER
2 EGG YOLKS

For the caramel glaze
125 G (4 OZ) SUGAR
2 TABLESPOONS WATER

Set the oven at gas mark 6 (200°C) 400°F.

Butter as many 20 cm (8 in) diameter sponge or flan tins as you have and dredge with flour. Non-stick tins or those with a moving flange are best. You will need five or six layers of cake, so you may need to bake more than one batch.

Beat the butter and sugar together until very light and fluffy.

Separate the eggs and beat in the yolks one by one.

Sift the flour with the baking powder and beat into the mixture.

Beat the whites with the pinch of salt until they stand in peaks but are not dry, and fold gently into the mixture.

Spread thin layers of the mixture – not more than $\frac{1}{2}$ cm ($\frac{1}{4}$ in) thick – into the cake tins and bake near the top of the oven for 8–10 minutes, until they are golden brown and set. Leave to cool a little then turn out on to wire racks. If you cannot bake all the layers at once, keep the mixture refrigerated between whiles.

Meanwhile make the chocolate cream. Melt the chocolate (see page 13), stir until smooth, then leave to cool a little. Boil the sugar and water together until a small amount dropped into cold water forms a soft ball – 116°C (240°F) on a sugar thermometer. Remove from the heat and leave to cool also.

Beat the butter until it is very soft and light, then beat in the melted chocolate. Beat in the syrup drop by drop, as for making mayonnaise (the syrup must not melt the butter), then beat in the egg yolks one by one. Refrigerate the cream until needed.

When all the cake layers have been cooked and cooled, select the smoothest and most perfect.

For the glaze, bring the sugar and water to the boil together and watch very carefully. As soon as the syrup turns a rich golden brown, remove from the heat, allow to cool for about one minute, then pour very carefully over the selected cake, making sure it is completely covered, but as far as possible not allowing the caramel glaze to flow over the edge.

Leave till almost set, then with a long sharp knife, mark into sections, cutting right through the caramel.

Now spread each of the other cake layers with a generous

coating of the chocolate cream (the layers of cream should be of about the same thickness as the cakes) and pile one on top of the other.

Top with the caramel-glazed cake, and spread any remaining cream round the sides.

CHOCOLATE CHEESE CAKE

For the base
225 G (8 OZ) PLAIN CHOCOLATE DIGESTIVE BISCUITS OR
    GINGER NUTS
125 G (4 OZ) BUTTER
25 G (1 OZ) SUGAR

For the cake
15 G (½ OZ) GELATINE
JUICE OF 1½ LEMONS
3 EGGS
500 G (1 LB) CREAM CHEESE OR 250 G (8 OZ) CREAM CHEESE
    AND 250 G (8 OZ) CURD CHEESE
50 G (2 OZ) SUGAR
150 ML (¼ PINT) DOUBLE OR WHIPPING CREAM
50 G (2 OZ) BITTER OR SEMI-SWEET CHOCOLATE
1 TABLESPOON DOUBLE OR SOURED CREAM

Crush the biscuits with a rolling pin. Melt the butter and add
the biscuit crumbs and the sugar. Stir over a gentle heat and
blend well, then spread evenly over the bottom of a 25 cm
(10 in) diameter springform tin or a china flan dish. Press
down firmly to make a smooth base for the cake.

Sprinkle the gelatine over the lemon juice in a small
saucepan and leave to soak. Separate the eggs.

Beat the cheese till smooth, then beat in the egg yolks and
the sugar. Beat until very smooth and light.

Heat the gelatine gently until it has completely dissolved,
then beat into the cheese mixture.

Whip the cream until thick but not stiff, and blend in.

Whisk the egg whites to a soft peak (do not allow to
become dry) and fold in.

Pour the mixture into the cake tin or flan dish, smoothing down the top.

Melt the chocolate (see page 13) and blend in the cream. Dribble the chocolate in a spiral pattern over the top of the cake and leave to set.

Refrigerate for at least 2 hours before serving.

CHOCOLATE NUT GÂTEAU

150 G (5 OZ) PLAIN OR BITTER CHOCOLATE
225 G (8 OZ) HAZELNUTS, WALNUTS OR UNBLANCHED
ALMONDS
50 G (2 OZ) PLAIN FLOUR
100 G (4 OZ) SUGAR
175 G (6 OZ) BUTTER
5 EGGS, SEPARATED
PINCH OF SALT
1 TABLESPOON CASTER SUGAR
For the filling
100 G (3½ OZ) PLAIN OR BITTER CHOCOLATE
300 ML (½ PINT) WHIPPING CREAM

Set the oven at gas mark 4 (180°C) 350°F.

Melt the chocolate in a large bowl (see page 13) and leave to cool a little.

Grind the nuts finely and blend with the flour, or put nuts, flour and 1 tablespoon of the sugar into a blender or food processor and blend together until the nuts are finely ground.

Cut the butter into small pieces and add to the chocolate in the large mixing bowl and beat well together. Add remaining sugar and beat until light and fluffy, then add the egg yolks one by one. Blend in the nut and flour mixture.

Beat the egg whites with the pinch of salt until they begin to stand in peaks, then beat in the caster sugar and whisk until they stand in firm peaks. Fold into the mixture.

Pour into a greased and floured 23 cm (9 in) diameter cake

tin, preferably a springform, and bake for 40–45 minutes, until the top is firm and the cake has shrunk slightly from the sides of the tin.

Leave to cool for 10 minutes in the tin, then turn out on to a wire cake rack.

To make the filling, melt the chocolate (see page 13) and leave to cool.

Whip the cream lightly and blend in the chocolate.

When the cake is quite cold, slice it in half and sandwich together with some of the chocolate cream, then cover the top and sides with remaining cream. Decorate if you like with chocolate leaves or curls (see page 292).

CHOCOLATE PUMPERNICKEL TORTE

You can use dark rye bread instead of the pumpernickel for this surprisingly light but crunchy dessert cake.

6 EGGS
175 G (6 OZ) SUGAR
4 TABLESPOONS RUM OR SHERRY
PINCH OF SALT
100 G (3½ OZ) PUMPERNICKEL
125 G (4 OZ) CHOCOLATE
25 G (1 OZ) WALNUTS OR HAZELNUTS
For serving
300 ML (½ PINT) WHIPPING CREAM
1–2 TEASPOONS SUGAR
2 TEASPOONS RUM OR SHERRY (OPTIONAL)

Set the oven at gas mark 5 (190°C) 375°F.

Separate the eggs and whisk the yolks with half the sugar until they are thick and foamy.

Whisk in the rum or sherry.

Whip the whites with the pinch of salt until they begin to stand in peaks, then slowly beat in the remaining sugar and continue to whisk until you have a stiff, glossy meringue mixture.

Grate or chop the pumpernickel, the chocolate and the nuts finely, or put them all into a blender or food processor together and reduce to fine crumbs.

Blend this mixture into the yolks, then gently but thoroughly fold into the whites.

Pour into a well-greased 23 cm (9 in) diameter springform tin and cook for 50–60 minutes, or until the top of the cake is firm and springy to the touch. Watch carefully for the last 5 or 10 minutes that the top does not burn.

Turn off the oven and leave the cake to cool in the oven with the door left open. It will sink rather as it cools, but don't worry.

Turn out of the tin and serve with the lightly whipped, slightly sweetened cream, laced if you like with a little rum or sherry.

The Manufactory, Bristol

CHOCOLATE ANGEL FOOD CAKE

A mere whisper of a cake, this needs light, quick handling, but once you have mastered the technique you will find this an excellent way of using up extra egg whites.

Serve plain, with fruit or ice cream, or use the marvellous icing given here, which is almost as light as the cake.

25 G (1 OZ) CORNFLOUR
70 G (2½ OZ) PLAIN FLOUR
2 TABLESPOONS COCOA POWDER
225 G (8 OZ) CASTER SUGAR
½ LEMON
10 EGG WHITES
2 PINCHES OF SALT
1 TEASPOON CREAM OF TARTAR

For the icing
50 G (2 OZ) PLAIN OR BITTER CHOCOLATE
40 G (1½ OZ) BUTTER
100 G (4 OZ) ICING SUGAR
4 TABLESPOONS MILK
1 EGG
PINCH OF SALT
A FEW DROPS VANILLA ESSENCE
50 G (2 OZ) FLAKED ALMONDS (OPTIONAL)

Set the oven at gas mark 4 (180°C) 350°F.

Have ready a 25 cm (10 in) diameter springform cake tin, using the base with the central funnel, or use a ring mould of similar capacity. Do not butter the tin, but flour it lightly.

Sift the cornflour, flour, cocoa and half the caster sugar together into a bowl and re-sift twice more to make them really light. Hold the sieve as high over the bowl as possible when sifting.

Rub 2 large bowls with the cut surface of the lemon, and divide the egg whites between them. Add a pinch of salt and a squeeze of lemon juice to each and begin to whisk one at a time. A copper bowl and balloon whisk are ideal; an electric mixer with a balloon whisk is also excellent. The main thing is that as much air as possible should be incorporated into the whites. When they begin to foam, add half the cream of tartar and continue to whisk until they stand in firm peaks. Then whisk in half the remaining caster sugar.

Repeat with the second bowl of egg whites. You should end up with a very stiff meringue mixture. Now transfer both lots of whites into the largest bowl you have, making sure first that the dish is free of grease. The idea is to provide as much surface as possible, so even a deep serving platter or a clean, cool work surface will do.

Sift some of the flour and cocoa mixture over the top of the whites, covering the surface only lightly, and fold in carefully, using a stiff spatula or a metal spoon. Work very delicately but thoroughly, and repeat until all the flour mixture has been incorporated.

Turn the mixture into the prepared cake tin, and run a knife through once to make sure there are no large air bubbles. Smooth the top.

Bake in the centre of the oven for 40–45 minutes, or until the top of the cake feels firm but springy.

Remove from the oven and invert over a wire cake rack which you have lifted off the table by standing it on four tins. This allows for maximum air circulation.

Only when the cake has completely cooled, slip a knife around the edge if necessary and remove from the tin.

To make the icing, melt the chocolate (see page 13). When it has melted, add the butter and stir until the mixture is quite smooth.

Put the remaining ingredients into a bowl and whisk lightly till smooth. Add the chocolate and butter and continue to whisk until the mixture is very thick, bulky and smooth (a good 5 minutes with an electric beater at maximum speed).

Slice the cake in half when quite cold, sandwich with rather less than half the icing, then spread the remaining icing thickly all over the cake with a palette knife.

Sprinkle the top and sides with the lightly toasted flaked almonds if you wish.

DEVIL'S FOOD CAKE

A really dark, rich and moist cake, with a thick fudgy icing.

125 G (4 OZ) PLAIN OR BITTER CHOCOLATE
150 ML (¼ PINT) WATER
125 G (4 OZ) BUTTER
225 G (8 OZ) SOFT BROWN SUGAR
2 EGGS
225 G (8 OZ) FLOUR
½ TEASPOON BAKING POWDER
PINCH OF SALT
150 ML (¼ PINT) SOURED CREAM

For the chocolate fudge icing
150 ML (¼ PINT) SINGLE CREAM OR MILK
50 G (2 OZ) PLAIN OR BITTER CHOCOLATE
100 G (3½ OZ) SUGAR
50 G (2 OZ) BUTTER
¼ TEASPOON VANILLA ESSENCE

Set the oven at gas mark 4 (180°C) 350°F.

Melt the chocolate with the water (see page 13). Stir until smooth and leave to cool.

Cream the butter and sugar together until light and fluffy. Add the eggs, one at a time, and beat until very light and smooth.

Blend in the melted chocolate.

Sift the flour with the baking powder and salt and beat into the mixture alternately with the soured cream. Pour into two buttered and floured 23 cm (9 in) diameter sponge tins and bake for 25–30 minutes. Leave to cool a little, then turn out on to a wire rack.

To make the icing, put the cream or milk into a small saucepan, break in the chocolate, add the sugar and melt over a moderate heat. When the chocolate and sugar have melted, bring to the boil and boil, stirring well, until the mixture thickens and a small amount, dropped into cold water, forms a soft ball, or a sugar thermometer registers 116°C (240°F).

Remove from the heat, add the butter cut into pieces, and the vanilla, and stir until smooth. When the mixture has cooled a little, beat vigorously with a wooden spoon until it has thickened sufficiently to spread. Sandwich the two cakes together with half the icing, and spread remaining icing over the top.

Men working at a primitive cocoa mill, van Houten's factory at Amsterdam, 1828

CHOCOLATE MILLE FEUILLES

Very simple and quick to prepare with ready-made puff
pastry.

225 G (8 OZ) PUFF PASTRY
For the filling
125 G (4 OZ) PLAIN OR BITTER CHOCOLATE
2 TABLESPOONS WATER
I TABLESPOON BRANDY
300 ML (½ PINT) DOUBLE OR WHIPPING CREAM –
   OR A LITTLE LESS
For the icing
SQUEEZE LEMON JUICE
HOT WATER
2 TABLESPOONS ICING SUGAR

Set the oven at gas mark 7 (220°C) 425°F.

Roll out the pastry into a rectangle ¼ cm (⅛ in) thick, then
cut it into three equal rectangles. Lift each individual rectangle of pastry up and slap it down flat on to the pastry board
several times, then roll out again to the original thickness.
This allows the pastry to shrink before, rather than during,
the baking.

Place each sheet on to a dampened baking tray and bake
in the centre of the oven for 15–20 minutes, or until well risen
and pale brown. Do not allow to get too dark, or it will taste
bitter.

Leave to cool on wire baking trays.

Meanwhile prepare the filling. Melt the chocolate with the

water and the brandy (see page 13). Stir until smooth and leave to cool.

Whip the cream till light and bulky.

Prepare the icing by stirring the lemon juice and enough hot water, a few drops at a time, into the icing sugar to make a smooth paste, just thick enough to spread easily.

When the pastry sheets have cooled, trim them if necessary to equal size and shape, and spread the icing over one sheet. Drizzle three thin parallel lines of the chocolate sauce down the length of the iced sheet, then draw the back of a knife across the lines to make the characteristic mille feuilles design.

Spread half the cream over one of the other sheets and drizzle on half the remaining chocolate sauce. Mingle it slightly into the cream with the knife. Place the second pastry layer on top and repeat. Top with the iced pastry sheet.

CHOCOLATE ROULADE

A really light dessert cake.

For the cake
6 EGGS
200 G (7 OZ) CASTER SUGAR
I TEASPOON VANILLA SUGAR OR A FEW DROPS
    VANILLA ESSENCE
50 G (2 OZ) COCOA POWDER

For the filling
125 G (4 OZ) PLAIN OR BITTER CHOCOLATE
2 TABLESPOONS BRANDY OR WATER
300 ML (½ PINT) DOUBLE OR WHIPPING CREAM

Set the oven at gas mark 4 (180°C) 350°F.

Separate the eggs and whisk the yolks with the sugar and vanilla until light and pale.

Sift the cocoa and fold it in lightly.

Whisk the whites until stiff but not dry and fold carefully into the mixture.

Pour into a buttered Swiss roll tin, approximately 33 × 20 cm (13 × 8 in) and spread evenly.

Bake for 20–25 minutes, until the top is springy to the touch. Do not overcook.

Remove from the oven and allow to cool for 10–15 minutes in the tin, then turn out carefully on to a sheet of greaseproof paper. Leave to cool and, when almost cold, roll up with the paper like a Swiss roll.

To make the filling, melt the chocolate with the brandy

or water (see page 13) and stir until smooth. Leave to cool a
little, then open up the sponge roll and spread on the chocolate mixture.

Whip the cream lightly and spread thickly over the chocolate. Roll up again and place carefully on a serving dish or
platter.

You can decorate the roulade with more whipped cream
and chocolate flakes or curls (page 292), finely chopped nuts
or roasted almonds before serving if you wish.

FRANKFURTER KRANZ
Chocolate Buttercream and Praline Ring

A traditional German ring-shaped cake (the kind you will see in the window of any good *Konditorei*), filled with a smooth butter cream, sometimes coffee-flavoured, sometimes chocolaty, and always bristling with praline.

For the cake
175 G (6 OZ) BUTTER OR MARGARINE
175 G (6 OZ) SUGAR
3 EGGS
175 G (6 OZ) SELF-RAISING FLOUR
50 G (2 OZ) CORNFLOUR
¾ TEASPOON BAKING POWDER
2 TABLESPOONS MILK OR SOURED MILK
GRATED RIND OF I LEMON
JUICE OF ½ LEMON

For the cream
100 G (3½ OZ) PLAIN OR BITTER CHOCOLATE
175 G (6 OZ) UNSALTED BUTTER
75 G (3 OZ) ICING SUGAR
2 TABLESPOONS VERY STRONG BLACK COFFEE
2 TABLESPOONS BRANDY OR RUM
2 EGG YOLKS

For the praline
125 G (4 OZ) BLANCHED ALMONDS
125 G (4 OZ) SUGAR

Set the oven at gas mark 6 (200°C) 400°F.

Butter a 20 cm (8 in) diameter springform cake tin, using the base with the central funnel, or use a ring mould of similar size.

Cream the butter or margarine with all but 1 tablespoon of the sugar until very light and fluffy.

Separate the eggs and add the yolks one by one.

Sift the flour with the cornflour and baking powder, and add slowly, alternating with the milk.

Add lemon rind and juice.

Whisk the whites until they stand in soft peaks, then whisk in the remaining sugar. Fold carefully into the cake mixture and pour into the ring mould.

Bake for 40–45 minutes, until a skewer inserted into the cake comes out clean.

Remove from the oven, allow to cool a little, then turn out on to a wire tray and leave to cool.

Meanwhile make the butter cream. Melt the chocolate (see page 13) and leave to cool a little.

Cream the butter with the icing sugar until very light and fluffy. Add the coffee and the brandy or rum and then beat in the egg yolks.

Finally blend in the cooled chocolate.

Make the praline (see page 20) but do not allow it to become too dark for this recipe.

Crush the praline to a quite coarse but fairly even consistency. It is best not to do this in a blender or food processor, which will reduce it to a fine powder: put the praline in a plastic bag and use a meat mallet or rolling pin on a wooden board.

When the cake is ready, cut it horizontally twice to form three layers and sandwich together with the chocolate butter cream, using about half the quantity.

Spread remaining butter cream over the cake, covering it completely, then sprinkle generously with the praline so that the ring is completely encrusted.

CHOCOLATE NEST

This is a curious recipe – half cake, half sunken soufflé, and infinitely more delicious than that sounds. It should be made on the day of serving.

Decorated with small Easter eggs, this makes an ideal Easter cake.

225 G (8 OZ) PLAIN OR BITTER CHOCOLATE
2–3 TABLESPOONS BRANDY OR LIQUEUR
I TABLESPOON VERY STRONG BLACK COFFEE
175 G (6 OZ) UNSALTED BUTTER
175 G (6 OZ) SUGAR
6 EGGS

For decoration (optional)
SMALL SUGAR OR FOIL-WRAPPED EASTER EGGS

Set the oven at gas mark 7 (220°C) 425°F.

Melt the chocolate with the brandy or liqueur and the coffee (see page 13). Stir until smooth then leave to cool a little.

Cream the butter with all but I tablespoon of the sugar until very light and fluffy.

Separate the eggs and beat in the yolks one by one.

Blend in the chocolate and stir until the mixture is quite smooth.

Set aside about one quarter of the mixture, to be used as a chocolate butter cream.

Whisk the egg whites until they stand in soft peaks, then beat in the remaining sugar until you have a stiff, glossy meringue. Fold this carefully but thoroughly into the remaining chocolate mixture and pour into a greased 25 cm (10 in) diameter cake tin, preferably a springform one.

Place in the hot oven and, after 10 minutes, lower the heat to gas mark 5 (190°C) 375°F and cook for a further 20–25 minutes, or until a skewer inserted into the centre just comes out clean.

Remove from the oven, leave to cool in the tin for 10 minutes, then remove the sides of the tin very carefully and leave the cake to cool on a wire rack. It will certainly sink in the centre, but don't be alarmed, as this will make the centre deliciously moist, and give the cake the necessary nest shape.

When the cake is quite cold, spoon the chocolate butter cream into the centre, and decorate with the eggs.

DR. NANSEN'S POLAR EXPEDITION — Messrs. Cadbury have supplied about 1,500. lbs. of Cocoa Essence and Chocolate in hermetically sealed tins. Dr. Nansen has exercised a wise choice in selecting an absolutely pure cocoa of such typical excellence as Cadbury's and one that contains the largest amount of nutriment in the smallest compass. Vide Press

SCHWARZWÄLDER KIRSCHTORTE
Black Forest Cherry Gâteau

A delicious rococo fantasy of dark chocolate cake, tart morello cherries and whirls of whipped cream.

150 G (5 OZ) PLAIN OR BITTER CHOCOLATE
2 TABLESPOONS WATER
150 G (5 OZ) UNSALTED BUTTER
150 G (5 OZ) CASTER SUGAR
4 EGG YOLKS
50 G (2 OZ) SELF-RAISING FLOUR
5 EGG WHITES
PINCH OF SALT
A 450 G (I LB) CAN MORELLO CHERRIES IN SYRUP
I DESSERTSPOON CORNFLOUR
I TABLESPOON KIRSCH OR BRANDY
300 ML (½ PINT) WHIPPING CREAM
I TEASPOON ICING SUGAR
25 G (I OZ) CHOCOLATE CURLS (SEE PAGE 292)

Set the oven at gas mark 6 (200°C) 400°F.

Butter a 20–25 cm (8–10 in) diameter cake tin with a removable bottom, preferably a springform tin. Dredge with flour until evenly covered, then shake out excess flour.

Melt the chocolate with the water (see page 13) and stir until quite smooth. Leave to cool a little.

Meanwhile beat the butter with the sugar until pale and fluffy. Beat in the yolks one by one and then beat in the flour. Blend in the chocolate.

Whisk the whites with the pinch of salt until they stand in soft peaks. Blend one third of the whites into the chocolate mixture until thoroughly amalgamated, then add the chocolate mixture to remaining whites and blend in gently but thoroughly.

Pour into the prepared cake tin and cook in the centre of the oven for 40–45 minutes, or until a skewer inserted into the centre just comes out clean. Turn off the oven and pull the cake to the front. Leave with the door open for five minutes, then remove from the oven, remove sides of the tin and leave to cool for another 15 minutes before sliding off the base on to a wire tray. Even with these precautions the cake will still sink a little, but this only makes it more delicious.

Cut in half horizontally when quite cold.

To make the filling, drain the cherries and stone them if necessary.

Measure out 150 ml ($\frac{1}{4}$ pint) of the cherry syrup, mix a tablespoon of it into the cornflour to make a smooth paste, bring the rest to the boil and pour in the cornflour mixture. Cook over moderate heat, stirring, until the sauce thickens. Leave to cool, then blend in half the kirsch or brandy.

Blend the rest of the kirsch or brandy with one tablespoon of the remaining cherry syrup and drizzle this over the bottom half of the cake.

Whip the cream with the icing sugar till quite stiff and spread half over the bottom cake layer. Spread the cherry sauce evenly over the cream and sprinkle on all but twelve of the cherries. Cover with the top layer of the cake.

Spread or pipe the remaining cream over the top, making twelve cream whirls round the edge. Dot each whirl with a cherry, and sprinkle the whole with the chocolate curls.

CHOCOLATE MARJOLAINE GÂTEAU

Rich and crunchy, and beautiful to look at with its many different coloured layers; a truly festive gâteau for a special occasion.

For the cake
225 G (8 OZ) ALMONDS
125 G (4 OZ) HAZELNUTS
225 G (8 OZ) CASTER SUGAR
1 TABLESPOON FLOUR
1 TABLESPOON COCOA POWDER
8–10 EGG WHITES (DEPENDING ON THE SIZE OF THE EGGS)

For the cream
225 G (8 OZ) SUGAR
150 ML (¼ PINT) WATER
225 G (8 OZ) UNSALTED BUTTER
3 TABLESPOONS BRANDY
3 EGG YOLKS
50 G (2 OZ) BITTER CHOCOLATE
6 TABLESPOONS PRALINE (SEE PAGE 20)
1 TABLESPOON VERY STRONG BLACK COFFEE

Set the oven at gas mark 6 (200°C) 400°F.

Butter and flour four 20–25 cm (8–10 in) diameter round baking tins, or two very large Swiss roll tins.

Blanch the almonds and roast or toast the hazelnuts until the skins are loose and can be blown off (out of doors or into the sink). Then roast or toast both together until they are golden brown.

Grind the nuts together finely and blend evenly with all but 2 tablespoons of the sugar and all the flour and cocoa. If you have a food processor, put all these ingredients in together and reduce to a fine powder.

Beat the egg whites until they stand in stiff peaks, then slowly beat in the remaining sugar until you have a dense, stiff meringue.

Sprinkle on a little of the nut mixture and fold in with a metal spoon or spatula. Continue until all the nuts have been folded in.

Divide the mixture evenly between the baking tins and smooth the tops. Bake for 10–15 minutes until lightly browned and firm. Remove from the oven, leave to cool a little then turn out of the tins on to wire cake racks and leave to cool. If you have used two Swiss roll tins, cut the cakes in half.

To make the butter cream, boil the sugar and water together until a small amount dropped into cold water forms a soft ball, or a sugar thermometer registers 116°C (240°F). Remove from the heat and leave to cool.

Meanwhile beat the butter until soft and light, and when the syrup has cooled beat it in drop by drop, as for making mayonnaise (the syrup must not melt the butter). Then beat in the brandy and egg yolks alternately.

Melt the chocolate (see page 13).

Divide the cream into three parts, one rather greater than the others. Beat about half the praline powder into the larger amount of cream, the melted chocolate into one of the smaller amounts, and the coffee into the remainder.

To assemble, place one of the cakes on a serving dish and spread thickly with the chocolate cream. Place another cake on top and spread with the coffee cream. Top with the third

cake and spread with two-thirds of the praline cream. Top
with the last cake, spread thinly with the remaining praline
cream and sprinkle with the rest of the praline powder.

ULTIMATE CHOCOLATE CAKE

The most densely chocolaty of them all, this is really a dessert gâteau, about which one correspondent rapturized 'you feel that your tongue has reached to the very soul of chocolate'.

Do not bother to make this unless you can use the very best quality bitter or semi-sweet dessert or cooking chocolate; if you cannot obtain unsweetened chocolate, use pure cocoa.

This cake will feed 4–6; double the quantities once you are confident and use a 25 cm (10 in) springform tin.

250 G (9 OZ) BITTER OR COOKING CHOCOLATE (SEE ABOVE)
25 G (1 OZ) UNSWEETENED CHOCOLATE OR COCOA
    POWDER (SEE ABOVE)
2 HEAPED TEASPOONS INSTANT COFFEE POWDER
2 TABLESPOONS RUM
50 G (2 OZ) ICING SUGAR
1 DESSERTSPOON CORNFLOUR
3 LARGE OR 4 MEDIUM EGGS
A FEW DROPS VANILLA ESSENCE
150 ML ($\frac{1}{4}$ PINT) DOUBLE CREAM

For serving (optional)
150 ML ($\frac{1}{4}$ PINT) WHIPPING CREAM
A FEW DROPS VANILLA ESSENCE

Heat the oven to gas mark 4 (180°C) 350°F.

Prepare a 23 cm (9 in) diameter, 5 cm (2 in) deep sponge or flan tin by buttering and flouring it liberally, then line with a few strips of butter paper.

Melt both chocolates together with the coffee dissolved in

2 tablespoons hot water and the rum (see p. 13). Stir till smooth and leave to cool.

Blend the cornflour into the icing sugar together with cocoa if you are using it, and sift together twice.

Beat the eggs together lightly with the vanilla essence, thoroughly blend in the icing sugar mixture and whisk with a balloon whisk, preferably with an electric beater, until they are very thick and foamy, and have at least trebled in volume.

Blend in the cooled chocolate mixture.

Whip the cream lightly and fold in carefully.

Pour into the prepared tin and bake in the centre of the oven for about one hour, or until a skewer inserted comes out clean. Turn off the oven, leave the door open and leave to cool. The cake will sink as it cools. Turn out of the tin and serve, if you like, with the lightly whipped, vanilla flavoured cream.

C. J. van Houten

COCOA BECOMES COCOA AND CHOCOLATE BECOMES CHOCOLATE

If chocolate has a hero, or a patron saint, it must be the nineteenth-century Dutchman, Coenraad J. van Houten, founder of the flourishing chocolate manufacturing company that still bears his name.

Up to the time of van Houten, chocolate had been made by grinding the roasted cocoa bean into a 'chocolate liquor', and combining it with sugar and spices. This was then brewed into a thick, rich, grainy beverage. But the cocoa bean consists of about 53 per cent fat, some of which could be extracted by the use of a hand press. A little would separate, float on the surface of the cup and could be spooned off, but most of the fat remained in the brew. To counteract the fattiness, chocolate manufacturers added farinaceous substances, such as flour, cornmeal (the Indians had used ground maize), oatmeal, arrowroot, or even dried acorns or dried lichen, as in a preparation known as Iceland Moss, which was being marketed well into the 1860s.

The breakthrough came in 1828, when van Houten invented a press which could extract about two thirds of the fat (or cocoa butter) from the bean, leaving a cake of a dry, powdery substance. At a stroke, he had invented cocoa as we now know it and opened the way for the invention of eating chocolate. It took nearly another twenty years before the firm of Joseph Fry, of Bristol, discovered how to combine the cocoa butter that had been extracted with chocolate liquor and sugar, to make the first eating chocolate.

Van Houten went further. He remembered hearing that the Mexican Indians sometimes added wood ash to their chocolate, claiming that this imbued it with extra health-giving properties. He realized that the active ingredient in wood ash must be potash and began to add this to his cocoa powder, thus making it more digestible still by neutralizing the acid – a process still known as 'dutching' the cocoa.

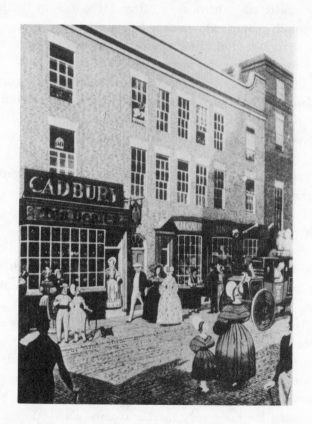

Meanwhile, in England, the tax on cocoa had been brought down. Although it was still more expensive than coffee or tea, it was no longer a rich man's drink. An advertisement in the radical journal, *The Poor Man's Guardian*, on 10 November 1832, shows how far cocoa (or 'theobroma' – food of the gods – as the advertiser calls it after the botanical name given to the plant by the eighteenth-century Swedish botanist, Carl von Linné), had sunk in the social scale.

THEOBROMA! – J. Cleave begs to call the attention of his Friends and the Public to the above new beverage, sold only by him, at 2d per pint. Its balsamic and nutritious properties render it peculiarly wholesome, and its cheapness advantageous to the working classes.

A major influence in the development of the chocolate industry in England were the Quakers, with their zeal for temperance. Whereas in the eighteenth century they had been prominent in the manufacture of beer, which was then a temperance drink (as opposed to gin and other spirits), in the nineteenth century they turned to the distribution of tea, coffee and cocoa, and later the manufacture of chocolate.

In 1824, the twenty-three-year-old John Cadbury opened a tea and coffee business next door to his father's draper's shop in Birmingham, where he was also 'desirous of introducing "Cocoa Nibs", prepared by himself, an article affording a most nutritious beverage for breakfast'. The cocoa proved unexpectedly popular and in 1831 he rented a small factory for producing just cocoa, moving into an even larger one in 1847, after he had taken his brother Benjamin into the business. The firm of Cadbury Brothers was born, to become one of the great chocolate family dynasties, combining, like

Fry's and Rowntree's, entrepreneurial genius with a passion for social reform.

By an ironic twist of history the Quakers, in becoming cocoa merchants, were later to find themselves embroiled in the slave trade. At the turn of the nineteenth century, they became aware of the disgraceful conditions under which the 'cocoa slaves' were coerced from their homes and forced to work on plantations in the Portuguese African colonies. It shows the power that the great Quaker chocolate manufacturers – Cadbury's and Rowntree's foremost among them – had by this time acquired, that they were able not only to impose a voluntary boycott in England on cocoa produced in these areas, but also to rally the support of the German and American chocolate firms.

A CHOCOLATE CURE FOR THWARTED LOVE

Recent research has shown that there is a chemical in chocolate, also found in the human brain, called phenylethylamine, which is directly related to the emotional highs and lows of being in love, and is a natural substance similar to amphetamines. People who become severely depressed over unrequited love – or who are suffering from hysteroid dysphoria, to give their condition its clinical name – often have a history of amphetamine abuse, and also often go on wild chocolate orgies when in a down state. According to one of the researchers, there is no other food as high in phenylethylamine as chocolate. 'It is speculative – highly speculative – that their chocolate bingeing might be an unconscious attempt at self-medication.'

Opposite, the Menier chocolate factory at Noisiel, from an engraving, 1867

ESTABLISHED IN 1780.

W. BAKER & CO.

PREMIUM CHOCOLATE

COCOA BROMA

DORCHESTER, MASS.

OFFICE 26 SOUTH MARKET STREET, BOSTON, MASS.

AND FOR SALE BY ALL THE PRINCIPAL GROCERS IN THE UNITED STATES.

These articles, to which first Premiums have been awarded by the chief Institutes and Fairs of the Union, are an excellent diet for children, invalids, and persons in health; allay, rather than induce, the nervous excitement attendant upon the use of tea or coffee, and are recommended by the most eminent physicians. Being manufactured from Cocoa of the best kind and quality, they are warranted equal, if not superior to any other Chocolates made in the United States, and may be returned if found unequal to the recommendation.

AGENTS.

D. C. MURRAY, New York.	KENNETT & DUDLEY, Cincinnati.	LOCKWOOD, WARD & CO., Troy.
GRANT & TWELLS, Phil'a.	WM. BAGALEY & CO., Pittsburg.	VOSE BROTHERS, New Orleans.
THOS. V. BRUNDIGE, Balt.	WAIT & COATES, Albany.	S. H. HOWELL, Georgetown, D. C.

CHAPTER

6

SMALL CAKES, BISCUITS AND COOKIES

W. BAKER & CO.'S EXHIBITION AT THE CRYSTAL PALACE. (1851)

BROWNIES

Brownies are an American classic – as corny as blueberry pie. Everyone has their own favourite recipe, and the controversy has even reached the pages of *Private Eye*, where a correspondent writes that 'brownies should be fudgy and nutty and disgustingly yummy'. On that at least everyone can agree and there is also a general consensus that true brownies can only be made with unsweetened cooking chocolate. What better recipe to give then, than the one put out by the makers of Baker's Cooking Chocolate themselves, for though I have tried many different recipes, and found them all delicious, this is certainly one of the best.

110 G (4 OZ) UNSWEETENED COOKING CHOCOLATE
50 G (2 OZ) UNSALTED BUTTER
75 G (3 OZ) PLAIN FLOUR
GOOD PINCH BAKING POWDER
GOOD PINCH SALT
2 EGGS
175 G (6 OZ) SUGAR
1 TEASPOON VANILLA ESSENCE
50 G (2 OZ) PECANS OR WALNUTS

Set the oven at gas mark 4 (180°C) 350°F.

Melt the chocolate (see page 13) and, when cooled a little, add the butter cut into small pieces. Stir until the butter has melted and blended with the chocolate.

Sift the flour with the baking powder and salt.

Beat the eggs together with the sugar and vanilla until fluffy and blend in the chocolate and butter mixture.

Fold in the flour and then the roughly chopped nuts.

Pour into a greased 20 cm (8 in) square baking tin and bake for 20–25 minutes, or until a skewer inserted just comes out clean.

Allow to cool, then cut into squares – they will turn fudgy as they cool.

VARIATION: MARBLED BROWNIES Use 50 g (2 oz) chocolate only; melt and set aside. Melt butter separately. Proceed as above until flour and nuts have been folded into butter and eggs. Divide mixture in half, add chocolate to one half. Pour first chocolate, then white mixture into baking tin, draw a knife through to 'marble' them, and bake as above.

*　　*　　*　　*　　*　　*　　*　　*　　*

*
The chocolate bar is an edible American flag, a
security blanket for the distraught, a barometer of   *
a nation's economic health.
*   *

The New York Times, Sunday, 25 February 1979

*　　*　　*　　*　　*　　*　　*　　*　　*

CHOCOLATE BUTTERSCOTCH BROWNIES

50 G (2 OZ) UNSALTED BUTTER
175 G (6 OZ) SOFT BROWN SUGAR (DARK OR LIGHT, OR A
    MIXTURE OF THE TWO)
2 EGGS
75 G (3 OZ) PLAIN FLOUR
GOOD PINCH BAKING POWDER
GOOD PINCH OF SALT
50 G (2 OZ) CHOCOLATE CHIPS
50 G (2 OZ) PECANS OR WALNUTS

Set the oven at gas mark 4 (180°C) 350°F.

Melt the butter together with the sugar over a moderate heat, until the sugar begins to caramelize. Set aside and leave to cool a little.

Beat the eggs until light and fluffy, then beat in the caramelized sugar mixture.

Sift the flour with the baking powder and salt and fold in, together with the chocolate chips and the roughly chopped nuts.

Pour into a greased 20 cm (8 in) square baking tin and bake for 20–25 minutes, or until a skewer inserted just comes out clean.

Allow to cool, then cut into squares.

CHOCOLATE COOKIES

125 G (4 OZ) PLAIN OR BITTER CHOCOLATE
125 G (4 OZ) BUTTER
1 EGG
175 G (6 OZ) GRANULATED OR SOFT BROWN SUGAR
175 G (6 OZ) SELF-RAISING FLOUR

Set the oven at gas mark 6 (200°C) 400°F.

Melt the chocolate (see page 13), leave to cool a little, then add the butter cut into pieces and stir until smooth.

Break the egg into a bowl. Add the sugar and stir in with a fork. Blend in the melted chocolate and butter mixture and then work in the sifted flour to make a stiff dough.

Roll the dough into balls each the size of a large walnut and place, well spaced, on a buttered or non-stick baking sheet.

Bake for 10–12 minutes, until they have spread out into round cookies, and the top of each is cracked like parched earth.

Remove from the oven and leave to cool and crisp on a wire tray.

CHOCOLATE CHIP COOKIES

Another American classic, much cheaper and infinitely more 'moreish' when made at home. It is easiest to use ready-made chocolate chips, but a good plain eating chocolate cut into small chips will also do.

125 G (4 OZ) BUTTER
50 G (2 OZ) SOFT PALE BROWN SUGAR
50 G (2 OZ) GRANULATED SUGAR
1 EGG
FEW DROPS VANILLA ESSENCE (OPTIONAL)
150 G (5 OZ) FLOUR
½ TEASPOON BICARBONATE OF SODA
PINCH OF SALT
125 G (4 OZ) CHOCOLATE CHIPS
50 G (2 OZ) WALNUTS OR PECANS

Set the oven at gas mark 5 (190°C) 375°F.

Beat the butter with both sugars until pale and fluffy, then beat in the egg and the vanilla essence.

Sift the flour with the bicarbonate of soda and the salt and beat into the mixture.

Stir in the chocolate chips and the finely chopped nuts.

Place small spoonfuls of the mixture on to well greased or non-stick baking tins, leaving plenty of room for the cookies to spread.

Bake for 10–15 minutes, until the little heaps have spread into thick cookies and are just beginning to turn golden brown.

Lift off the baking sheets and leave to cool and harden on a wire cake rack.

COUNTRY CRUNCH BARS

These crunchy uncooked chocolate bars are child's play to make, and everyone's pleasure to eat.

50 G (2 OZ) BUTTER OR MARGARINE
200 G (7 OZ) PLAIN CHOCOLATE
3 TABLESPOONS GOLDEN SYRUP
225 G (8 OZ) PLAIN DIGESTIVE OR RICH TEA BISCUITS
ICING SUGAR

Put butter, chocolate and golden syrup in a small heavy saucepan and heat gently, stirring until all the ingredients have melted and are thoroughly blended.

Break the biscuits into quite small pieces and stir into the mixture.

Pour into a greased shallow tin, approximately 18 cm (7 in) square and refrigerate for several hours till set.

Turn out of the tin, cut into bars and dust each bar lightly with icing sugar.

A PERSONAL REMINISCENCE

A personal reminiscence: during the war, when I was a little boy, my father settled me on a farm. One day the War Agricultural Committee or Milk Marketing Board sent us a stern letter saying that our cows' milk was deficient in 34% of non-fatty solids (or some such %). We, or rather the farmeress, wrote back asking what the – was *she* supposed to do about it. Within days a great sack arrived, full of *cow-chocolate*. Great, fist-sized nuggets of rock-hard black chocolate, studded with coarse sugar crystals like pyrites. The cows got some of it. I was not a very happy child at the time but I vividly remember happy afternoons in the hay-loft, devouring a great bound volume of the *Boy's Own Paper* (c. 1890) and gnawing at the rock-hard cow-chocolate. You had to spit out the bits of sacking-thread embedded in it. Sweetmeats were rare in those days. It was two or three years after the war, I fancy, that the Labour Government abolished the rationing of sweets. The abolition started on a Sunday, to buffer the effect, I suppose. I was making a long bus journey on that day and recall that every sweet shop was open and besieged, not by kids but by fat ladies, buying chocolate and toffee by the cwt. The *Daily Mirror* next day excelled itself: most of the front page was taken up by an enormous headline: '*GREEDY-GUTS!*' Rationing went on again almost immediately.

From a letter to the author from Kyril Bonfiglioli

CHOCOLATE ALMOND CRESCENTS

Light and crisp little biscuits, which are good with coffee, tea or after-dinner drinks. You can make them in a number of different ways – plain and half-dipped in chocolate, you can add cocoa to the mixture and dust the finished biscuits with icing sugar, or you can also dip the cocoa-flavoured biscuits in chocolate. These quantities allow you to make all three variations with one basic mixture.

225 G (8 OZ) UNSALTED BUTTER
65 G (2½ OZ) CASTER SUGAR
1 EGG YOLK
1 GOOD TEASPOON BRANDY
125 G (4 OZ) ALMONDS
65 G (2½ OZ) CORNFLOUR
225–275 G (8–10 OZ) PLAIN FLOUR
1 TABLESPOON COCOA POWDER

To finish
50 G (2 OZ) ICING SUGAR
100 G (3½ OZ) PLAIN OR BITTER CHOCOLATE
1 TABLESPOON FLAVOURLESS VEGETABLE OIL

Set the oven at gas mark 4 (180°C) 350°F.

Cream the butter with the caster sugar until the mixture is very white and fluffy.

Beat in the egg yolk and the brandy.

Blanch the almonds if necessary, and grind them in a blender or food processor. This is better than using ready-ground almonds which are too fine, and do not give the biscuits their characteristic crunchiness. Beat the almonds into the butter and sugar mixture.

Sift the cornflour with 225 g (8 oz) of the flour and beat in. Add a little more flour if necessary to make a dough that is just stiff enough to shape.

Using half this basic mixture, break off walnut-sized pieces of dough and, with lightly floured hands, roll each one into a fat little sausage shape with pointed ends and form into a crescent as you place them on buttered or non-stick baking sheets.

Beat the cocoa into the remaining basic mixture and form into crescents in the same way.

Bake for 25–30 minutes. The biscuits should be firm and just beginning to colour, no more.

Remove to a wire tray and allow to cool a little.

Take half the cocoa-flavoured biscuits and roll them in the icing sugar while still warm. Leave to cool and store in an airtight box or tin, powdered with the remaining icing sugar.

Melt the chocolate with the oil (see page 13) and stir until smooth. Dip the remaining white and brown biscuits into the chocolate so that only one horn of each crescent is coated. Leave on wire trays until the chocolate has set, then store also in airtight tins or boxes.

PINWHEELS

Plain biscuits with a difference, these are pretty to look at and fun to make.

225 G (8 OZ) FLOUR
PINCH OF SALT
125 G (4 OZ) SUGAR
50 G (2 OZ) GROUND ALMONDS
125 G (4 OZ) BUTTER
2 EGG YOLKS
1 TEASPOON VINEGAR
1 TABLESPOON COCOA POWDER

Sift flour, salt, sugar and ground almonds on to the pastry board, dot with the butter cut into small pieces, make a well in the centre and put in the yolks and vinegar. Using a palette knife, cut and mix until the mixture resembles fine bread-crumbs.

A food processor, of course, makes light work of this. Simply put in all the above ingredients and process together.

Now divide the mixture in half. Gather up one half and knead lightly into a smooth dough. Cut once to make sure it is really smooth and set aside on a plate.

Sift the cocoa over the remaining mixture and gather and knead this also into a smooth dough. It is particularly important to cut this in half to make sure the cocoa is evenly distributed and there are no flecks of white. Gather into a ball and leave both doughs in a cool place for one hour.

Set the oven at gas mark 6 (200°C) 400°F.

Roll out both doughs separately into rectangles, just under ½ cm (¼ in) thick. Cut each into strips about 10 cm (4 in) wide and 20 cm (8 in) long. Place a strip of chocolate dough on to a strip of white dough and roll them up together lengthwise into smooth sausage shapes. Chill again, then cut across into whirls about ¾ cm (⅓ in) thick.

Place the biscuits on buttered or non-stick baking sheets and bake near the top of the oven for 8–10 minutes.

Remove on to a wire baking tray and leave to cool.

CHOCOLATE LEBKUCHEN
Spiced Honeycakes

The gabled medieval town of Nürnberg, home of the Meistersinger and birth place of Albrecht Dürer (and of the author), is famous also for its *Lebkuchen*. These spiced honeycakes, of which there are many varieties, are an essential part of a German Christmas.

Though the exact recipes for the *echt* (true) Nürnberger Lebkuchen are a closely guarded secret, the following are a good enough imitation and very delicious, and they are a great pleasure to make, as the whole house begins to smell of Christmas while they are baking.

This recipe is for the basic, rather dry *Lebkuchen* or honeycake, which comes in many different shapes and sizes, not only rounds, squares and lozenges, but also heart shapes, often highly decorated and iced with loving messages. Chocolate-lovers will agree that a plain chocolate icing is the best.

Make these *Lebkuchen* several weeks in advance, and store them in a cool dry place. They are very dry and hard at first, but become softer in time.

350 G (12 OZ) HONEY
125 G (4 OZ) SUGAR
25 G (1 OZ) BUTTER
450 G (1 LB) FLOUR
1 SCANT TEASPOON GROUND CINNAMON
SCANT ¼ TEASPOON GROUND CLOVES

125 G (4 OZ) BLANCHED ALMONDS
50 G (2 OZ) CANDIED PEEL
¼ TEASPOON CREAM OF TARTAR
1 TABLESPOON MILK
1 EGG

For icing

125 G (4 OZ) PLAIN OR BITTER CHOCOLATE

Put the honey, sugar and butter into a heavy saucepan and stir over a gentle heat until melted and smooth.

Sift the flour with the spices.

Chop the nuts and peel together very finely.

Dissolve the cream of tartar in the milk and stir into the lightly beaten egg. Pour the contents of the saucepan into a large mixing bowl and add remaining ingredients in turn, bit by bit, working them in with a wooden spoon until you have a smooth mass. Gather the dough into a ball and leave in a cool place overnight.

The following day, heat the oven to gas mark 6 (200°C) 400°F.

Roll out the dough on a lightly floured board to ½ cm (¼ in) thickness and cut into 6–8 cm (2½–3 in) rounds, or other shapes, with a biscuit cutter, or use the rim of a glass.

Place on well-buttered or non-stick baking sheets and bake for 15–20 minutes, or until lightly browned on top.

Remove from the baking sheets and leave on a wire tray to cool.

When quite cold, melt the chocolate (see page 13) and spread a thin smooth covering of chocolate on each *Lebkuchen*, using a knife or palette knife.

NOTE: You can also use this mixture to make a gingerbread house.

Bake it in shallow baking trays and cut the sheets into shapes to construct a house. Decorate with coloured icing, non-pareils and chocolate drops.

★   ★   ★   ★   ★   ★   ★   ★   ★

★   'When you have breakfasted well and fully, if you will drink a big cup of chocolate at the end you will have digested the whole perfectly three hours later, and you will still be able to dine.'   ★

★   J.-A. Brillat-Savarin, *Physiologie du goût, 1825*   ★

★   ★   ★   ★   ★   ★   ★   ★   ★

ELISEN LEBKUCHEN

These are lighter, nuttier and much less chewy than the previous recipe. They are always made in large circles, and may be left plain or iced with a pink or white sugar icing, but chocolate devotees will insist on the chocolate icing. They are exported all over the world from Nürnberg in highly decorated, traditional drum-shaped tins.

These too should be made a week or two before Christmas, and stored in airtight tins. If rice paper is unobtainable, use buttered foil; peel off when the *Lebkuchen* are cool and firm enough to handle.

175 G (6 OZ) ALMONDS, *not* BLANCHED
50 G (2 OZ) MIXED CANDIED PEEL
3 EGG WHITES
250 G (9 OZ) CASTER SUGAR
2 TEASPOONS GROUND CINNAMON
$\frac{1}{4}$ TEASPOON GROUND CLOVES
GOOD SQUEEZE LEMON JUICE
FINELY GRATED PEEL OF $\frac{1}{2}$ LEMON
RICE PAPER

For the icing
50 G (2 OZ) PLAIN OR BITTER CHOCOLATE
BLANCHED ALMONDS, HALVED (OPTIONAL)

Grind the almonds very finely and chop the peel finely.

Whisk the egg whites until they stand in peaks, then gradually whisk in the sugar, until you have a smooth dense mass.

Beat in the ground almonds, the finely chopped peel, the spices and lemon juice and peel, and mix well.

Place the rice paper on baking sheets and, using a dessert-spoon, make mounds of the mixture, well spaced apart. Smooth each one out to form a circle 6–8 cm (2½–3 in) in diameter.

Leave to dry at room temperature for a few hours or overnight.

Bake in a moderate oven, gas mark 3 (160°C) 325°F for 40–50 minutes until a smooth pale crust has formed on top, but the inside, if you break the crust, is still a little tacky.

Remove from the oven, and leave to cool on a wire baking tray, breaking off any excess rice paper.

When quite cold, melt the chocolate (see page 13) and spread smoothly over the top of each *Lebkuchen*. You can also decorate the top with blanched almond halves pressed in to form a pattern.

CHOCOLATE LIGHTNING THINS

The 'lightning' refers to the speed with which these are made and eaten.

125 G (4 OZ) BUTTER OR MARGARINE
125 G (4 OZ) SUGAR
2 EGGS
100 G (3½ OZ) FLOUR
2 TABLESPOONS COCOA POWDER
50 G (2 OZ) ALMONDS
I TEASPOON GROUND CINNAMON
I TABLESPOON SUGAR

Set the oven at gas mark 6 (200°C) 400°F.

Cream the butter or margarine with the sugar until light and fluffy. Beat in the eggs one by one, then beat in the flour and cocoa, sifted together.

Spread thinly on a buttered 34 × 24 cm (13 × 10 in) baking sheet, or on several smaller ones – the mixture should not be more than ½ cm (¼ in) thick. Flake the almonds or chop them fairly finely, and scatter evenly over the top.

Blend the cinnamon into the sugar and sprinkle on evenly.

Bake for 20 minutes near the top of the oven, so that the almonds become lightly browned. Remove from the oven, leave to cool for a few minutes only, then cut into small squares or lozenge shapes and leave on a wire tray to cool. They will become quite crisp when cold, and should preferably be eaten on the day of making.

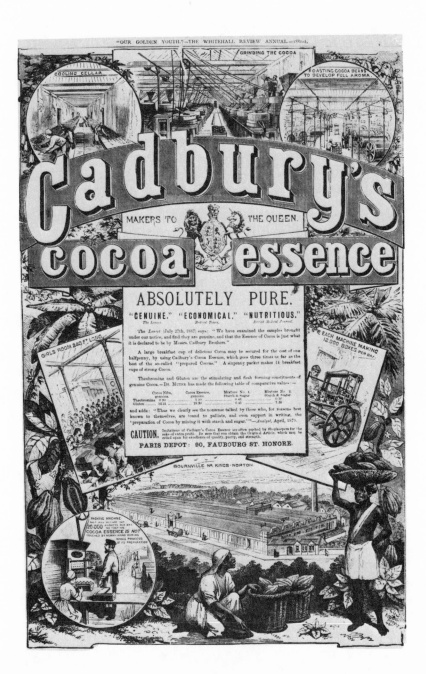

CHOCOLATE MACAROONS

These little macaroons may be made with almonds or with hazelnuts, and the latter give a particularly rich flavour. They are delicious on their own, or served as petits fours with ice cream or other desserts.

They can be made in two different ways, which give surprisingly different results. Method 1 makes dark, slightly moist macaroons, while the macaroons made by method 2 have a light and crisp outside, and are dark and fudgy in the centre.

125 G (4 OZ) ALMONDS OR HAZELNUTS
50 G (2 OZ) PLAIN OR BITTER CHOCOLATE
2 EGG WHITES
PINCH OF SALT
75 G (3 OZ) CASTER SUGAR
RICE PAPER (OPTIONAL)

Set the oven at gas mark 4 (180°C) 350°F.

Blanch the almonds and roast or toast them until golden brown.

If you are using hazelnuts, roast or toast them. This not only improves the flavour, but also detaches the skins, which can then be blown off (best done in the sink or out of doors).

METHOD I

Leave the nuts to cool, then grate or grind them finely. Melt the chocolate (see page 13) and leave to cool. Whisk the egg whites with the salt until they begin to stand in peaks, then slowly add the sugar. Whisk until the meringue is very stiff and glossy.

Blend in the cooled melted chocolate and fold in the ground nuts.

METHOD 2

When the nuts are cool, grate or grind them finely. Grate the chocolate finely also. If you have a food processor, you can put nuts and chocolate in together.

Make the meringue mixture as described above and fold in the nuts and chocolate.

FOR BOTH METHODS

Line baking sheets with rice paper or buttered foil or use non-stick tins. Drop on teaspoonfuls of the mixture in small mounds, and bake for 15–20 minutes.

Remove from the oven, allow to cool a little, then break away excess rice paper or peel off foil; leave on a wire tray to cool.

SPICED CHOCOLATE
MACAROONS

Very light, and more fragile than the previous recipe, these are half-way between a meringue and a macaroon, and are an excellent accompaniment to ices, mousses or other desserts.

50 G (2 OZ) PLAIN OR BITTER CHOCOLATE
3 EGG WHITES
175 G (6 OZ) CASTER SUGAR
I TEASPOON GROUND CINNAMON
PINCH OF GROUND CLOVES
75 G (3 OZ) GROUND ALMONDS
RICE PAPER (OPTIONAL)

Heat the oven to gas mark 4 (180°C) 350°F.

Melt the chocolate (see page 13) and leave to cool.

Whisk the egg whites until they begin to stand in peaks, then slowly beat in the sugar until you have a dense, shiny meringue mixture.

Blend the spices into the ground almonds, sift these over the meringue and fold in carefully. Blend in the cooled melted chocolate.

Line baking sheets with rice paper, or, if this is unobtainable, with lightly buttered foil, or use non-stick baking sheets.

Put dollops of the mixture on the baking sheets with a dessertspoon, leaving plenty of space between each as they will spread a good deal.

Bake in the centre of the oven for 40–50 minutes. The

macaroons should have a pale crusty top, but still be a little moist in the centre.

Leave to cool a little, then remove from the baking trays and cut or break away excess rice paper, or peel off the foil.

Leave on wire baking trays to cool and harden.

Portrait, by the Swiss artist Jean-Étienne Liotard, of Anna Baltauf, the original *'Belle Chocolatière'* (see also page 306)

CHOCOLATE MERINGUES

This mixture can be used to make individual meringues, to be sandwiched together with ice cream or lightly whipped cream (flavoured with alcohol, or more chocolate, if you like); miniature meringues for decorating desserts or large cakes; or large meringue circles to be served as beautiful party desserts, sandwiched together and decorated with any number of fillings (see below).

150 G (5 OZ) ICING SUGAR
40 G (1½ OZ) COCOA POWDER
5 EGG WHITES
150 G (5 OZ) CASTER SUGAR

Set the oven at gas mark 1 (140°C) 275°F.

Prepare some baking sheets by covering closely with foil. Butter the foil and sprinkle lightly with sifted flour. Knock off any excess.

Sift the icing sugar and cocoa together. Whisk the egg whites, slowly at first, and then at top speed. When the whites begin to reach the soft peak stage, add the sifted cocoa and sugar slowly while continuing to beat.

When the mixture is quite stiff, fold in the caster sugar gently but thoroughly, using a metal spoon or a spatula.

To make individual meringues, make nicely rounded mounds on the prepared baking sheets, using two table-spoons, or a pastry bag with a 1 cm (½ in) nozzle. For tiny meringues, use a ½ cm (¼ in) nozzle, or two teaspoons. To make meringue circles, use the 1 cm (½ in) nozzle, and pipe the circle, starting at the outside and spiralling towards the centre. You can also smooth the mixture into circles, using a metal spatula. This amount should make 2 circles of 20–24 cm (8–10 in) diameter.

Place in the prepared oven and cook for at least 1 hour. The miniature meringues will probably be done by that time, the larger individual ones and the circles will take at least $1\frac{1}{2}$ hours.

Leave to cool a little, then peel off very carefully from the foil and leave on wire trays to cool.

If the meringues are not quite done, or still a little tacky on the bottom, return them to the oven, upside down if the bottoms are sticky, for up to a further half hour.

The meringues may be stored in airtight tins or, carefully wrapped and protected against damage, in the freezer. They can be used almost instantly when removed from the freezer.

To make a party dessert, sandwich the two circles together and cover the top with any of the following. You can also decorate them with miniature meringues or meringue mushrooms, or chocolate flakes, curls or leaves (see page 292).

1 Whipped cream, only very lightly sweetened, and laced, if you like, with brandy, rum, kirsch or liqueur.

2 Chocolate cream: melt 100 g ($3\frac{1}{2}$ oz) plain or bitter chocolate (see page 13) and leave to cool a little. Whip 300 ml ($\frac{1}{2}$ pint) whipping cream lightly and blend in the chocolate.

3 Raspberry cream – this is a particularly delicious combination: Sweeten 125 g (4 oz) raspberries lightly and crush or blend. Sieve the purée and fold into 300 ml ($\frac{1}{2}$ pint) lightly whipped cream. (Frozen raspberries are excellent for this.)

4 Rich Chocolate Mousse (see page 76). This makes a particularly rich dessert. The meringues must be made first,

as the mousse must be spread as soon as it is ready and before it sets.

5 Ice cream of any flavour. Soften the ice cream a little and assemble just before serving.

NOTE: To make meringue mushrooms for use as decoration: omit the cocoa from the meringue mixture, and put the mixture into a piping bag with 1 cm (½ in) nozzle.

Pipe small rounds, to make the mushroom caps, and an equal number of thick stumps. If your meringue mixture is very firm, you can hold the nozzle 2 cm (1 in) above the baking tray, and cut off the meringue at the nozzle leaving a straight, upstanding stump on the tray; if the mixture is not stiff enough for this, pipe sausage shapes about 2 cm (1 in) long on to the baking sheet, leaving one end slightly pointed.

When the meringues are cooked, press a small indentation in the bottom of each cap and push in a stump, cementing it with a little whipped cream or icing. Dust the caps lightly with cocoa, and dip the base of the stems in cocoa to simulate soil.

Opposite, eighteenth-century chocolate house in Leipzig, engraving by A. Bernigroth

FLORENTINES

These are a little bit tricky to make at first, but so delicious that it is worth mastering the technique. Once you have done so, you will find them quite quick and simple to make. Store in airtight tins.

225 G (8 OZ) ALMONDS
175 G (6 OZ) MIXED CANDIED PEEL
50 G (2 OZ) GLACÉ CHERRIES
50 G (2 OZ) BUTTER
175 G (6 OZ) CASTER SUGAR
25 G (I OZ) PLAIN FLOUR
300 ML (½ PINT) DOUBLE CREAM
225 G (8 OZ) PLAIN OR BITTER CHOCOLATE

Set the oven at gas mark 5 (190°C) 375°F.

Blanch the almonds and chop them. They may be chopped unevenly, so that some are fine and others are left quite chunky.

Chop the candied peel and the glacé cherries fairly finely.

Melt the butter and sugar together in a heavy saucepan over a moderate heat, stirring constantly and on no account allowing it to brown. When the mixture is fairly liquid (the sugar will not melt completely at this temperature) add the flour and continue to stir over a gentle heat until the mixture is quite smooth and comes away clean from the sides of the pan. Watch carefully that it does not brown.

Slowly add the cream, stirring well to keep the mixture

smooth, then remove from the heat and add the almonds and fruit. Stir well.

Drop teaspoonfuls of the mixture on to buttered and floured or non-stick baking tins, leaving plenty of space between.

Place near the top of the oven and cook for 10–12 minutes, until they have spread and are lightly browned at the edges. Remove from the oven. At this point the florentines are still very malleable. If they have spread out too much and so will break too easily, or if indeed they have become merged with one another, it is easy to manoeuvre them back into shape with the tip of a palette knife.

Leave to cool for 3 minutes on the baking sheets, then remove to a wire tray and leave to cool.

Melt the chocolate (see page 13) and thickly coat the flat side of each florentine, and place it, chocolate side up, on a tray or work surface. When all the florentines have been coated, make wavy lines on the chocolate with a fork. Leave to cool and set.

PAINS AU CHOCOLAT
Chocolate Croissants

A favourite *goûter* for the French child returning from school, these are made from the same dough as croissants, and hence retain the name in English, but they are usually oblong in shape, like a large sausage roll.

Though the process is rather lengthy, they are fun to make.

10 G (SCANT ½ OZ) FRESH YEAST
2 TABLESPOONS WARM WATER
25 G (1 OZ) SUGAR
250 G (9 OZ) STRONG WHITE BREAD FLOUR
1 TEASPOON SALT
150 ML (¼ PINT) MILK
1 TABLESPOON CORN OIL
100 G (3½ OZ) BUTTER
125 G (4 OZ) PLAIN OR BITTER CHOCOLATE

For the glaze
1 EGG YOLK
2 TABLESPOONS MILK

Dissolve the yeast in the warm water with 1 teaspoonful of sugar. Leave in a warm place until frothy.

Sift 225 g (8 oz) of the flour into a warm bowl with the salt, make a well in the centre and pour in the yeast mixture. Warm the milk with the remaining sugar and the oil, and add it also.

Gently blend the flour into the liquid, then turn out on to a floured board and knead very lightly, just until the dough begins to keep its shape. Use a plastic spatula if the mixture is too soft to knead by hand. Return the dough to the clean mixing bowl, cover with a cloth and leave in a fairly warm place for 3–4 hours until it has risen to about three times its original volume.

Knock the dough down and leave to rise again for 1–2 hours, or until it has doubled in bulk.

Have the butter at room temperature, and when the dough is ready, flatten it between sheets of greaseproof paper by beating it gently with a rolling pin.

Knock the dough down in the bowl, place it on a lightly floured board and gently roll it into a rectangle three times as long as it is wide. Spread the butter over the two thirds of the rectangle furthest away from you, leaving a 1 cm ($\frac{1}{2}$ in) margin. Fold the unbuttered third towards the centre, and then fold over again. Seal the edges.

Give the dough a half turn and roll out again into a rectangle. Fold into three once more, wrap loosely in a lightly floured plastic bag and leave in the refrigerator for one hour.

Take out of the refrigerator, punch it down and leave for a few minutes at room temperature, then roll out into a rectangle and fold into three again. Replace in the refrigerator for at least another hour.

When the dough is ready, divide into half and roll out the first half on a lightly floured board into a rectangle just under $\frac{1}{2}$ cm ($\frac{1}{4}$ in) thick and approximately 15 cm (6 in) wide. Cut the dough into 15 cm (6 in) squares, and each square into two rectangles.

Chop the chocolate roughly and sprinkle a line of chocolate down the centre of each rectangle. Roll up like a sausage roll and place on to lightly greased baking sheets.

Repeat with the remaining dough.

Set the oven at gas mark 8 (230°C) 450°F.

Leave the prepared croissants in a warm place until they have risen to twice their size and feel springy to the touch.

Brush with a glaze made from the egg yolk mixed with the milk and bake for 15–20 minutes.

The prepared croissants may also be left in the refrigerator overnight. Leave at room temperature for half an hour before baking.

Neptune being handed a casket of chocolate so that he can make it known to the rest of the world; frontispiece of a text on chocolate, 1639

ÉCLAIRS

Finger-sized éclairs, light, elegant and not too sweet, are a tea-time classic.

For the éclairs
300 ML (½ PINT) WATER
100 G (3½ OZ) BUTTER
PINCH OF SALT
I TEASPOON SUGAR
125 G (4½ OZ) FLOUR
4 EGGS

For the filling
200 ML (⅓ PINT) DOUBLE OR WHIPPING CREAM
I TEASPOON ICING SUGAR

For the icing
4 TABLESPOONS WATER
I TABLESPOON SUGAR
50 G (2 OZ) PLAIN OR BITTER CHOCOLATE
I TEASPOON COFFEE POWDER
100 G (3½ OZ) ICING SUGAR
½ TEASPOON CORN OR TASTELESS SALAD OIL

Set the oven at gas mark 7 (220°C) 425°F.

Make the éclair mixture exactly as for making Profiteroles (see page 62), then fill the mixture into a piping bag with a plain 1 cm (½ in) nozzle, and pipe finger-sized éclairs on to buttered baking sheets, leaving plenty of space between each one. The éclairs should be slightly stumpy at each end.

Bake for 20–25 minutes, or until well risen and pale brown.

Remove from the oven and turn it off. Make an incision down the side of each éclair with a sharp, pointed knife to allow the air to escape, lay them on their sides on the baking sheets and return to the oven to dry for 10 minutes, leaving the oven door open. Then leave to cool on a wire rack.

Whip the cream with the icing sugar until light but firm, and fill the éclairs, using the piping bag, a knife or a teaspoon.

To make the icing, put the water and sugar in a small saucepan and bring slowly to the boil, stirring until the sugar has dissolved. Boil quite briskly for 1 minute. Remove from the heat and break in the chocolate. Stir until dissolved. Add the coffee and slowly beat in the icing sugar, keeping the mixture gently warm. Stir in the oil.

Using a knife, coat the top of each éclair thickly with the chocolate icing and leave to set before serving.

CAPTAIN SCOTT AT THE POLE - TAKING RECORDS.

RIGO JANCSI SQUARES

Half-way between cake and 'confection', these infinitely delicious creamy chunks are said to have been named after a nineteenth-century gypsy violinist, who was as seductive as the cake that bears his name. He broke hearts wherever he went, until finally a princess ran away with him, causing a great scandal. A clever Hungarian chef created the cake to immortalize the romance.

Time-consuming and very expensive in chocolate, but not really difficult to make, they can be served for a very special tea-time occasion, or as petits fours to end a feast.

For the cake
75 G (3 OZ) PLAIN OR BITTER CHOCOLATE
175 G (6 OZ) UNSALTED BUTTER
75 G (3 OZ) SUGAR
4 EGGS
PINCH OF SALT
I TABLESPOON CASTER SUGAR
50 G (2 OZ) SELF-RAISING FLOUR

For the filling
300 ML (½ PINT) DOUBLE CREAM
275 G (10 OZ) PLAIN OR BITTER CHOCOLATE
4 TABLESPOONS RUM
I TEASPOON VANILLA ESSENCE (OPTIONAL)

For the icing
225 G (8 OZ) SUGAR
150 ML (¼ PINT) WATER
200 G (7 OZ) PLAIN OR BITTER CHOCOLATE

Begin by making the cake.

Set the oven at gas mark 4 (180°C) 350°F.

Melt the chocolate (see page 13) and leave to cool.

Meanwhile, beat the butter with half the sugar until white and fluffy.

Separate the eggs and whisk the yolks with the remaining sugar until this mixture too is pale and bulky.

Combine the chocolate with the butter and then blend in the egg yolk mixture.

Whisk the whites with the pinch of salt until they begin to stand in peaks, then slowly beat in the caster sugar and continue to beat until they are stiff and glossy. Now add one third of the egg whites to the cake mixture and blend in well. Pile remaining egg whites on top, sift on the flour and, using a spatula, cut and fold into the mixture so that it becomes thoroughly blended, with no white streaks showing, but remains very light.

Pour into a well-buttered and lightly floured Swiss roll tin, and bake for 15–20 minutes, until a skewer inserted into the centre comes out clean, and the cake has shrunk away slightly from the sides. Leave to cool a little, then turn out on to a cake rack to cool completely.

Meanwhile, make the filling. Pour the cream into a small, heavy saucepan, break in the chocolate and stir over a gentle heat until the chocolate has dissolved and is well blended. Continue to simmer, stirring constantly, for 5–10 minutes until the mixture thickens. Then remove from the heat, pour into a mixing bowl, leave to cool and refrigerate for at least an hour.

When the mixture has set, beat in the rum and vanilla essence, and whisk lightly to make a smooth, light cream. Be careful not to overbeat.

When the cake has cooled, slice it in half horizontally and spread the chocolate cream thickly over one half. Top with the other half of the cake. The cream layer should be at least twice as thick as the cake layers. Refrigerate again.

Meanwhile, make the icing. Put the sugar and water into a heavy saucepan and bring slowly to the boil, stirring all the time until the sugar has dissolved. Allow to boil for one minute, then remove from the heat and break in the chocolate. Stir until the chocolate has completely melted. Leave to cool for 15–20 minutes, but do not allow the icing to set.

When the icing begins to thicken, pour it slowly and carefully over the cake, so that it completely covers the top without having to spread it, which would spoil the sheen.

Leave to cool and set for at least 2 hours in the refrigerator, then cut into small squares before serving.

CHOCOLATE CHESTNUT
SQUARES

This very rich cake can be eaten as a dessert or as a confection.
The mixture can also be shaped into a Yule log, lightly scored
with a fork to give the appearance of bark, sprinkled with
a little icing sugar to look like snow, and decorated with
hazelnuts to represent knots in the bark.

750 G (1½ LB) CHESTNUTS
125 G (4 OZ) CASTER SUGAR
125 G (4 OZ) PLAIN OR BITTER CHOCOLATE
100 G (3½ OZ) UNSALTED BUTTER
For the icing
125 G (4 OZ) PLAIN OR BITTER CHOCOLATE
1 TABLESPOON WATER
15 G (½ OZ) BUTTER

Peel the chestnuts by putting them into a large saucepan,
cover with cold water and bring to the boil. Boil for 10
minutes, then take off the heat and take the chestnuts out, a
few at a time, and peel off outer and inner skins, holding
them in a cloth if they are very hot.

When all the chestnuts have been peeled, put them into a
large heavy saucepan again, cover with cold water and
simmer for about 20 minutes, or until they are tender. Drain
and purée in a blender or food processor, or a mouli-légumes.

Fold the sugar into the purée and leave to cool.

Melt the chocolate (see page 13), stir until smooth, then add
the butter, cut into small pieces, and stir again till smooth.

Work this into the chestnut mixture until you have a soft, smooth mass.

Either turn into a greased cake tin and chill overnight, or chill the mixture, then form into a Yule log and leave overnight to set.

To make the icing, melt the chocolate with the water (see page 13). Add the butter and stir till smooth.

Spread over the chestnut mixture, leave to set, and cut into squares before serving, or decorate the Yule log as suggested above.

WALNUT AND CHOCOLATE SLICES

This recipe comes from one of the many walnut-growing areas of France, where every *pâtisserie* has its own walnut speciality.

225 G (8 OZ) SHORTCRUST PASTRY
50 G (2 OZ) UNSALTED BUTTER
100 G (4 OZ) WALNUTS
3 EGGS
2 TABLESPOONS HOT STRONG BLACK COFFEE
175 G (6 OZ) SOFT BROWN SUGAR
75 G (3 OZ) FLOUR

For the butter icing
50 G (2 OZ) UNSALTED BUTTER
175 G (6 OZ) ICING SUGAR
2 TABLESPOONS STRONG BLACK COFFEE

For the chocolate icing
125 G (5 OZ) PLAIN OR BITTER CHOCOLATE
1 TABLESPOON CREAM
15 G (1½ OZ) BUTTER

Set the oven at gas mark 5 (190°C) 375°F.

Line a 20 × 30 cm (8 × 12 in) cake tin with the pastry and bake blind for 15 minutes near the top of the oven.

Melt the butter gently till creamy and leave to cool.

Chop the walnuts quite finely.

Whisk the eggs with the hot coffee and the sugar until thick and fluffy. Gently fold in the butter and the sifted flour. Blend in the walnuts.

Pour this mixture into the pastry case and spread on evenly.

Return to the oven and bake for 25–30 minutes, until firm. Leave to cool.

To make the butter icing, beat the butter with the icing sugar and the coffee until smooth. Spread thinly over the cooled cake and chill to help the icing to set.

To make the icing, melt the chocolate in a small bowl (see page 13). Add the cream and stir over a pan of simmering water until smooth. Remove the bowl from the heat. Add the butter cut into small pieces and stir until melted and the mixture is smooth and shiny. Leave to cool, spread evenly over the cake and leave to set.

Cut into squares before serving.

Un Cavalier, et une Dame beuvant du Chocolat

'Ce jeune Cavalier et cette belle Dame se regalent de Chocolat;
Mais l'on voit dans leurs yeux une si vive flame
Qu'on croit qu'il leur faudroit un mets plus délicat.'

Is Chocolate an
Aphrodisiac?

The Peruvian Indians thought it was. Centuries later, Madame du Barry is said to have given chocolate to her lovers, and Casanova declared that he drank it instead of champagne.

Much of the ecclesiastic controversy that raged round chocolate in the seventeenth century centred on this point. The theologian Johannes Franciscus Rauch published a Disputation in 1624 in which he inveighed against the immoderate use of chocolate by the monks, claiming that it was a violent inflamer of passions, and that if monks had been forbidden to drink it, the scandals with which the holy order had been branded might have been groundless.

At about the same time the English physician, Henry Stubbs, writes of chocolate in *The Indian Nectar*:

And as *Chocolata* provokes other Evacuations through the feveral *Emunctories* of the body, fo it doth that of *Seed*, and becomes *provocative to lust* upon no other account ...

Havelock Ellis, the nineteenth-century authority on sex, took a similar view.

The belief that chocolate could stimulate waning sexual prowess died hard. Cocoa was one of the ingredients of the notorious eighteenth-century stimulant 'Spanish Fly' and references to its powers were numerous. An eighteenth-century German copper-plate shows an elderly couple, the wife offering a cup of chocolate to her husband, with the words:

> 'You drink, my love, and I'll enjoy it too.
> I offer it to you, together with my heart,
> For we must still give heirs unto the waiting world.'

It is true that caffeine and theobromine, both contained in chocolate, act as stimulants to the central nervous system, but by the twentieth century, chocolate seems to have lost its reputation as an aphrodisiac, and that modern authority, Norman Douglas, does not have a single recipe using chocolate in his *Venus in the Kitchen*. However, in the privately published *Paneros* he says:

Regarding chocolate, I judge it to be of neutral effect; a cloying product fit for serving maids; yet possessed of value as an endearment, an incentive working not upon body but upon mind; it generates, in those who relish it, a complacent and yielding disposition. Deprived of chocolate, your lover of serving maids is deprived of a persuasive helpmate.

German eighteenth-century copperplate (see opposite). The German above the couple reads 'Delectable in consumption, fruitful in evacuation.'

Joseph Fry

THE CHOCOLATE EXPLOSION

In the nineteenth century, developments of new techniques in the manufacture of chocolate and the invention of new confections, many of which are still household favourites today, came in a torrent. Here, in the form of a chronology, are some of the crucial dates:

A REMINDER FROM THE EIGHTEENTH CENTURY

1728 Walter Churchman opens the first factory in England for processing the cocoa bean, in Bristol, and is granted letters patent by George II.

1761 Joseph Fry purchases the patent from Walter Churchman.

1765 James Watt perfects his steam engine.

1765 John Hannon sets up a chocolate factory with Dr Baker in Massachusetts, USA.

1780 The first chocolate factory using steam-powered machines is opened in Barcelona.

THE NINETEENTH CENTURY

1819 François-Louis Cailler opens the first Swiss chocolate factory on Lake Geneva.

1824 John Cadbury opens a shop in Birmingham for the sale of coffee, tea and cocoa (see page 212).

1825 Jean Antoine Brutus Menier, manufacturer of pharmaceutical powders, adds some chocolate grinding machinery to his mill at Noisiel, on the Marne, in order to use excess water power. Noisiel is still the site of the Chocolat Menier works (now owned by Rowntree Mackintosh and today, incidentally, home of the Polo mint). By the 1870s, the factory was surrounded by a model town for the employees. '*Le chômage est inconnu à Noisiel, en raison des sacrifices faits par les patrons.*' An early example of the benevolent despotism of nineteenth-century chocolate manufacturers.

The original Menier chocolate factory at Noisiel, a perfect example of an early iron-frame building

1828   Coenraad van Houten files a patent for 'chocolat powder'.

1847   Messrs Fry and Sons make the world's first solid eating chocolate.

1853   A uniform tax of 1d a pound is imposed on cocoa in England, thus making it reasonably cheap.

1862   Henry Isaac Rowntree acquires a cocoa and chocolate business from another Quaker, William Tuke, in York.

1866   Cadbury's market 'Cocoa Essence', a pure cocoa with no additives, from which the excess cocoa butter has been extracted. Two years later Fry's follow suit.

> To adulterate Cocoa's become such a practice
> That really the State must step in to protect us,
> The faculty tell us to drink, but the fact is
> The stuff is so starched they can hardly expect us.
> Who wish for pure cocoa in all its quintessence
> Will certainly find it in Cadbury's Essence.

1866   Fry's introduce the Chocolate Cream Bar, still a best seller more than a century later.

1869   Harriet Beecher Stowe, in *The American Woman's Home or Principles of Domestic Sciences* says, 'Chocolate is a French or Spanish article, and one seldom served on American tables.'

1875   Daniel Peter (who was courting Fanny Cailler, daughter of François-Louis) used the condensed milk made by his compatriot, Henri Nestlé, to create the first milk chocolate.

1879 Cadbury's buy the Bournbrook Estate to build their Bournville factory found the garden suburb for their employees.

1880 Rodolphe Lindt, a Swiss chocolate manufacturer, discovered that by leaving a batch of chocolate to be mixed over several days, the texture was changed from grainy to smooth – and invented the process now known as 'conching'. At the same time he also added extra cocoa butter, which made the chocolate so smooth that it melted in the mouth – 'chocolat fondant' had been discovered.

THE TWENTIETH CENTURY

1900 Forty-three-year-old Milton Snavely Hershey sells his caramel factory to the American Caramel Company for one million dollars ('Caramels are a fad,' he said, 'chocolate is a permanent thing') and starts his chocolate factory, and model town, later to be called Hersheyville. 'It will be the biggest chocolate business in the world, you'll see,' he told his wife.

1905 Cadbury's Dairy Milk is launched.

1907 The Hershey Kiss is invented. They now tumble off the machines, fully wrapped and with their characteristic flag, at the rate of 1,300 per minute, per machine.

1910 Cadbury's Bournville Plain chocolate comes on the market.

1913 Jules Séchaud, Swiss chocolateer, produces the first filled chocolate.

1921 Cadbury's launch their Fruit and Nut Chocolate.

1923 Milky Way is invented by a Chicago confectioner.

1930 Fry's Crunchy and Cadbury's Whole Nut are launched.

1932 The Mars Bar is born, invented by Forrest Mars, son of the inventor of Milky Way. How many do they now produce per day? The firm is reluctant to give a precise number, but 'if you like to suggest a figure around two million, you would not be far wrong'.

1933 Black Magic chocolates are introduced after extensive market research which included questioning guests at 'one very superior garden party'.

1935 Aero chocolate comes on the market – it looked good value because of its air bubbles.

1936 Invention of the Malteser – tiny pieces of Horlicks-flavoured dough exploded in a vacuum, and chocolate coated. Originally launched as 'Energy Balls'.

1936 Quality Street chocolates are launched, named after a play by J. M. Barrie.

1937 Kit Kat, Rollo and Smarties all burst on the world.

1938 Cadbury's Roses chocolates are introduced.

1940 The U S army asks Hershey to develop a chocolate that could survive tropical climates in a soldier's pocket and sustain him when there was no other food; recalling Cortés' statement in 1521 that 'one cup ... allows a man to walk a whole day without taking nourishment'. After Pearl Harbor, 500,000 'Field Ration D' bars were produced every 24 hours.

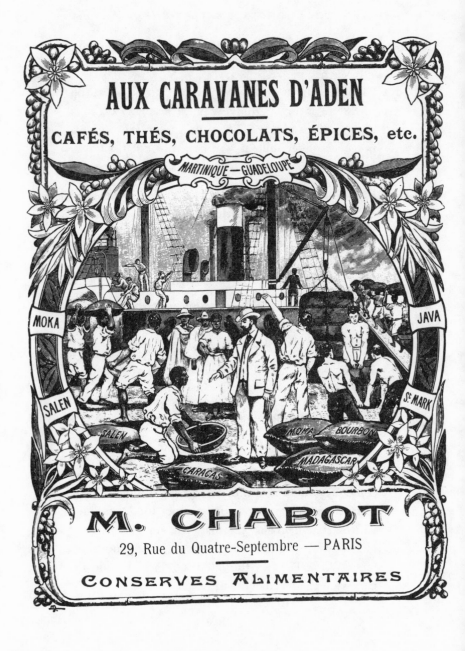

CHAPTER
7

CONFECTIONERY

Chocolate card by Henry Maillard, confectioner, 1097 Broadway,
New York

FRESH CREAM TRUFFLES

These really melt in the mouth and are equally good made with any of the flavourings suggested below. They must be kept in the refrigerator and should be eaten within two or three days.

150 ML (¼ PINT) THICK DOUBLE CREAM
1 VANILLA POD
1 EGG YOLK
25 G (1 OZ) CASTER SUGAR
150 G (5 OZ) PLAIN OR BITTER CHOCOLATE
25 G (1 OZ) UNSALTED BUTTER
1 TABLESPOON BRANDY, RUM OR LIQUEUR
   OR 1 TABLESPOON MODERATELY FINE PRALINE POWDER
     (SEE PAGE 20)
   OR 1 TEASPOON INSTANT COFFEE POWDER
COCOA POWDER
125 G (4 OZ) PLAIN CHOCOLATE
1 TEASPOON TASTELESS SALAD OIL

Bring the cream to the boil with the split vanilla pod. Remove from the heat, cover and leave to infuse.

Whisk the egg yolk with the sugar until pale and thick. Whisk into the cream and return to the heat very briefly to heat through, but on no account allow to boil. Remove from the heat again, take out the vanilla pod and add the chocolate. Stir until the chocolate has melted and blended into the cream.

Place in the refrigerator for about half an hour until set, but not completely hard, then remove from the refrigerator and, using a rotary or electric beater, whisk in the butter, which should be at room temperature, and the choice of flavouring.

Fill the mixture into a piping bag with a 1 cm ($\frac{1}{2}$ in) nozzle, and pipe small sausage shapes or balls on to a plate or sheet of foil.

Refrigerate for at least an hour until set quite hard.

Sift the cocoa on to a plate.

Melt the chocolate with the oil in a small container (see page 13) and leave to cool a little.

Using a dipping fork or a fine, two-pronged fork such as a fondue fork, or a fine skewer or two toothpicks, dip each truffle quickly in the melted chocolate and turn until it is coated on all sides, then roll immediately in the cocoa.

Refrigerate until ready to serve.

CHOCOLATE NUT TRUFFLES

These are very quick and simple to make with a blender or food processor. You can make them with any nuts of your choice – almonds, hazelnuts (or best of all, a combination of the two), pecans, walnuts, or even chestnuts.

Best eaten fresh, but will keep well in the refrigerator for up to 2 weeks.

125 G (4 OZ) NUTS, SHELLED WEIGHT
50 G (2 OZ) ICING SUGAR OR A LITTLE MORE, ACCORDING TO TASTE
125 G (4 OZ) PLAIN OR BITTER CHOCOLATE
25 G (1 OZ) UNSALTED BUTTER
4 TABLESPOONS COCOA POWDER

If you are using almonds, blanch them first.

Roast or toast almonds or hazelnuts until golden brown. Blow off the skin of hazelnuts after roasting. Chestnuts must first be cooked in water or milk until soft (see page 256).

If you have a food processor, put the nuts, icing sugar and chocolate – broken into pieces – in together and process until fine. Add the butter and process until the mixture is quite smooth and forms itself into a ball.

If you are using a blender, blend the nuts and icing sugar together until reduced to a fine powder. Grate the chocolate finely and blend into the nut and sugar powder. Soften the butter (but on no account melt it), and with a wooden spoon, beat into the mixture.

Chill the mixture for 10 minutes to firm it a little, then form balls or small sausage shapes and roll them in the cocoa.

Store in the refrigerator in an airtight box, and sprinkle with plenty of cocoa before storing, as they continue to absorb it.

NOTE: you can also coat the truffles in chocolate if you wish (see page 274).

Early-nineteenth-century chocolate advertisement

Chocolates

Once some people were visiting Chekhov.
While they made remarks about his genius
the Master fidgeted. Finally
he said, 'Do you like chocolates?'

They were astonished, and silent.
He repeated the question,
whereupon one lady plucked up her courage
and murmured shyly, 'Yes.'
'Tell me,' he said, leaning forward,
light glinting from his spectacles,
'what kind? The light, sweet chocolate
or the dark, bitter kind?'

The conversation became general.
They spoke of cherry centres,
of almonds and Brazil nuts.
Losing their inhibitions
they interrupted one another.
For people may not know what they think
about politics in the Balkans,
or the vexed question of men and women,

but everyone has a definite opinion
about the flavour of shredded coconut.

Finally someone spoke of chocolate filled with liqueur,
and everyone, even the author of *Uncle Vanya*,
was at a loss for words.

When they were leaving he stood by the door
and took their hands.
        In the coach returning to Petersburg
they agreed that it had been a most
unusual conversation.

Louis Simpson

QUICK TRUFFLES

Very light, and quick and easy to make. They are excellent coated in chocolate, but this is not essential.

Best eaten fresh, but may be stored in the refrigerator for up to two weeks.

125 G (4 OZ) PLAIN OR BITTER CHOCOLATE
125 G (4 OZ) UNSALTED BUTTER
125 G (4 OZ) ICING SUGAR
2 TEASPOONS INSTANT COFFEE POWDER (OPTIONAL)
2 TEASPOONS BRANDY, RUM OR LIQUEUR (OPTIONAL)

For coating
2 TABLESPOONS COCOA POWDER OR
  125 G (4 OZ) PLAIN OR BITTER CHOCOLATE
1 TEASPOON TASTELESS SALAD OIL

Melt the chocolate (see page 13). Leave to cool.

Beat the butter with the sugar until pale and fluffy.

Beat in the chocolate and the coffee and any spirits or liqueur.

Refrigerate the mixture for at least half an hour until it hardens enough to be rolled into balls or small sausage shapes.

Either roll these in cocoa, or melt the chocolate with the oil (see page 13) and coat each truffle in chocolate. Leave on foil to set.

COLETTES

This truffle mixture is so light that it is best piped into chocolate cases. Store in the refrigerator and eat very fresh — within two or three days.

275 G (10 OZ) PLAIN OR BITTER CHOCOLATE
½ TEASPOON FLAVOURLESS SALAD OIL
20 PETITS FOURS CASES
150 ML (¼ PINT) DOUBLE CREAM
1 TABLESPOON FLAVOURING — BRANDY, RUM OR LIQUEUR OR VERY FINELY CRUSHED PRALINE POWDER (SEE PAGE 20)

Melt 175 g (6 oz) of the chocolate with the oil (see page 13) and stir till smooth.

Using a teaspoon, spread the inside of the petits fours cases thinly with the chocolate and refrigerate.

Bring the cream just to boiling point, remove from the heat and add remaining chocolate. Leave for 5 minutes for the chocolate to melt, then stir until smooth and return to a moderate heat. Stir until the mixture just begins to bubble, then remove from the heat and leave to cool a little.

Now add the flavouring, a little at a time, and stir well. Leave to cool at room temperature for half an hour; if it still remains very soft, refrigerate for a short while.

When the cream begins to set, spoon into a piping bag with a small star nozzle and pipe into the chocolate cases.

Refrigerate until ready to serve. Serve in the paper cases — they should peel off quite easily.

CHOCOLATE ALMOND ROCKS

The burnt almond taste gives this simple confectionery a very sophisticated flavour.

125 G (4 OZ) BLANCHED ALMONDS
1 TABLESPOON SUGAR
225 G (8 OZ) PLAIN OR BITTER CHOCOLATE
25 G (1 OZ) UNSALTED BUTTER

Split the almonds in half, then cut lengthwise into thin slivers (this is the tedious part). Put them on a baking sheet, sprinkle with the sugar and toast under a hot grill until the sugar has melted and the almonds are medium brown. Shake the tin frequently to ensure even browning and be careful not to let them burn.

Melt the chocolate (see page 13) and remove from the heat. Add the butter and stir until smooth.

Add the toasted almonds and stir until they are evenly distributed in the chocolate.

Spoon small heaps of the mixture into paper petit-four cases, or on to non-stick baking sheets or a sheet of kitchen foil and leave to harden.

CHOCOLATE FONDANT CREAMS

Making fondant is messy and hard work, and it requires fine timing, but once you have mastered the skill you can make smooth, fine-textured fondant creams of whatever flavour you wish – peppermint, coffee, almond or fruit. Be sure to use only pure peppermint or fruit essences (obtainable from good grocers and chemists) – the artificial flavourings have a very coarse taste. You can also add a few drops of the appropriate food colouring if you wish.

Once you are confident in 'turning' the fondant, you can double the quantities given below, divide the mixture and, using different flavourings, make an assortment of creams, but it is best to practise with this amount first (any less is not worth working on).

500 G (1 LB) SUGAR
150 ML ($\frac{1}{4}$ PINT) WATER
SQUEEZE OF LEMON JUICE
GOOD PINCH CREAM OF TARTAR
FEW DROPS PEPPERMINT, ALMOND, COFFEE OR
    FRUIT ESSENCE
ICING SUGAR
125 G (4 OZ) BITTER CHOCOLATE
$\frac{1}{2}$ TEASPOON FLAVOURLESS SALAD OIL
FLAVOURING (SEE BELOW)

Put the sugar, water and lemon juice into a large heavy saucepan and bring slowly to the boil, stirring until all the sugar has dissolved. When the syrup begins to boil, add the cream of tartar and boil rapidly until it reaches 116°C (240°F) on a sugar thermometer, or until a small amount dropped into cold water forms a soft ball. If necessary, brush down the sides of the pan with a wet pastry brush from time to time to prevent the syrup from crystallizing.

When the right temperature has been reached, remove the pan from the heat and leave to cool for about 5 minutes.

Pour carefully on to a cool working surface (marble is ideal) and leave until a skin begins to form round the edge (10–15 minutes). Now begin to work the fondant. Using a wooden spoon or a wood or plastic spatula, work it backwards and forwards in a figure of eight motion. Scrape the

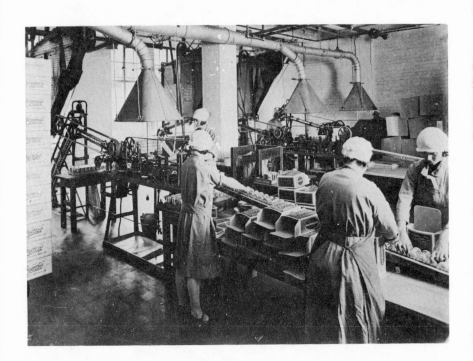

sides towards the centre from time to time, and keep the mixture together in as small an area as possible. Continue to work it in this way until it becomes opaque, white and quite firm. It will become progressively more difficult to work, but the more you work it, the finer the texture will be. It is also important not to work the fondant when it is too hot, as this makes it grainy.

When the mixture is ready, sprinkle the surface with a little icing sugar and knead in the chosen flavouring and colouring drop by drop, to taste. Continue to work with the wooden spoon or to knead by hand until the fondant is quite soft and pliable and comes away clean from the surface.

Sprinkle the surface with a little icing sugar and roll out the fondant approximately ½ cm (¼ in) thick. Cut into small rounds and leave to dry overnight on a wire baking tray.

If this proves difficult, line a baking sheet with foil and sprinkle it liberally with icing sugar. Drop on small dollops of fondant, or shape balls by hand into the size of large hazelnuts. Sprinkle them with more icing sugar and flatten them into discs with a knife or the back of a spoon. Leave to dry for some hours, then transfer to a wire rack and leave to dry out overnight.

Melt the chocolate with the oil (see page 13) and stir until smooth. Leave to cool a little. For peppermint or coffee creams, add a little sifted instant coffee powder to the chocolate coating; for almond or fruit creams, add some drops of bitter almond essence – the bitterer the chocolate in contrast to the sweetness of the fondant, the better.

Use a dipping fork or a fine two-pronged fork, such as a fondue fork, two toothpicks, or a fine skewer and dip each cream quickly in the chocolate until covered on all sides. Leave on a piece of foil to harden and peel off when set.

NOTE: You can also put aside some of the fondant, before flavouring it, to use for fondant icing or for dipping fruit.

It keeps very well in a screwtop jar in the refrigerator. Place the jar in a pan of hot water to melt the fondant before using.

TO USE AS ICING, colour and flavour it if you wish, then pour carefully over the cake, and leave to dry.

TO MAKE FONDANT-DIPPED FRUIT, melt the fondant as above, then quickly dip in individual fruits, such as cherries, firm strawberries, grapes, or segments of citrus fruit. The fruit must be absolutely perfect and dry for this, otherwise the juice will leak into the fondant and prevent it from hardening.

Allow excess icing to drip back into the jar, then leave to dry on foil. Eat very fresh.

These fondant fruits can subsequently be dipped in chocolate (see page 296).

QUICK CHOCOLATE FONDANT CREAMS

These can be literally child's play to make, and are very good provided you use a natural oil or essence of peppermint, coffee, almond or fruit, and not an artificial flavouring. They dry out rather quickly and should be eaten within a week.

450 G (1 LB) ICING SUGAR
PINCH CREAM OF TARTAR
1 EGG WHITE
WATER (SEE METHOD)
$\frac{1}{4}$–$\frac{1}{2}$ TEASPOON OIL OF PEPPERMINT OR OTHER FLAVOUR-
    ING (SEE ABOVE)
125 G (4 OZ) CHOCOLATE
$\frac{1}{2}$ TEASPOON FLAVOURLESS SALAD OIL

Sift 350 g (12 oz) of the icing sugar into a bowl with the cream of tartar and add the egg white. Work into a smooth paste adding water as needed, a teaspoonful at a time. Use some of the icing sugar that has been kept back if the mixture becomes too soft.

Add flavouring drop by drop until the required strength has been achieved. (All this can be done in a few moments in a food processor.)

Sprinkle half the remaining icing sugar on a board, flatten out the mixture and sprinkle with a little more icing sugar, then roll out to $\frac{1}{2}$ cm ($\frac{1}{4}$ in) thick and cut into rounds, about $2\frac{1}{2}$ cm (1 in) diameter. If you do not have a biscuit cutter of the right size, use the rim of a liqueur glass.

Leave on a wire tray overnight to dry out, then coat with chocolate melted with the oil as for the Fondant Creams.

CHOCOLATE GINGER OR CANDIED PEEL

This couldn't be simpler to make, but is a very sophisticated after-dinner confection, because it is not too sweet. It must be made from whole pieces of good quality crystallized stem ginger or candied peel, or a combination of the two.

225 G (8 OZ) CRYSTALLIZED STEM GINGER OR 225 G (8 OZ)
MIXED CANDIED PEEL
125 G (4 OZ) PLAIN OR BITTER CHOCOLATE
½ TEASPOON FLAVOURLESS SALAD OIL

Cut the ginger or peel into strips not more than 1 cm (½ in) wide.

Melt the chocolate with the oil (see page 13) in a small container, and stir until smooth.

Use toothpicks to dip each strip individually into the chocolate so that it becomes completely coated.

Put on greaseproof paper or foil to set. Peel off when the chocolate has hardened, and serve on a pretty, small dish, or put into paper petit four cases.

CANDIED PEEL AND NUT CONFECTION

Delicious, unusual and very quick and simple to make.

125 G (4 OZ) MIXED CANDIED PEEL
125 G (4 OZ) BLANCHED ALMONDS
2 EGG WHITES
125 G (4 OZ) ICING SUGAR
50 G (2 OZ) PLAIN OR BITTER CHOCOLATE

Chop the candied peel and the almonds together quite finely.

Combine the egg whites and icing sugar in a small heavy saucepan, add the peel and almonds and stir over a gentle heat until all is well blended and the mixture begins to cohere and becomes slightly shiny.

Remove from the heat and leave to cool a little.

When cool enough to handle, break off small pieces the size of a large hazelnut, and roll into balls or thin sausage or crescent shapes. Leave for a few hours to cool and set.

When the confection has hardened, melt the chocolate in a small bowl (see page 13) and dip in each piece, one by one, speared on a toothpick, until it is completely covered with chocolate.

Leave on a piece of foil or greaseproof paper to harden, and when set, peel off the foil or paper and place each on a dish or in a paper petit-four case.

CHOCOLATE FUDGE

Through many years of family fudge-making, this is the recipe that has proved the most consistently popular and successful, as well as requiring only the simplest of ingredients. However, it must be very carefully timed if the consistency is to come right.

300 ML (½ PINT) MILK
450 G (1 LB) SUGAR
25 G (1 OZ) COCOA POWDER
25 G (1 OZ) BUTTER
½ TEASPOON VANILLA ESSENCE
125 G (4 OZ) CHOPPED NUTS OR RAISINS (OPTIONAL)

Heat the milk with the sugar in a wide, heavy saucepan and stir until the sugar has dissolved. Add the cocoa and butter and bring slowly to the boil, stirring continuously so that the mixture becomes quite smooth. Continue to stir and boil until a temperature of 116°C (240°F) is reached on a sugar thermometer, or until a small amount of the mixture dropped into a glass of cold water forms a soft ball and does not make the water cloudy. This may take as much as 10–15 minutes, and the last few minutes are crucial as unless the correct temperature has been reached the fudge will not set. If it is exceeded, it will turn into toffee.

As soon as it reaches the 'soft ball' stage, remove the saucepan from the heat, add the vanilla and continue to stir or beat with a wooden spoon. When the mixture begins to thicken, add any chopped nuts or raisins you wish to use. Continue to beat until the mixture loses its gloss and becomes really thick and silky. Pour immediately into a buttered tin and leave in a cool place to set.

Cut into squares when set.

CHOCOLATE DECORATION AND OTHER FRIVOLITIES

Since one cannot have too much of a good thing, most cakes and desserts can be further embellished by chocolate decorations. I have not specified these in the recipes unless they are part of the classic presentation of the dish, as I do not want the reader to be put off by unnecessary complications; but when you have the time or inclination, there is no end to the number of ways, simple or elaborate, in which you can use chocolate to beautify your creations.

Any of these decorations may be stored in a rigid container in a cool place, ready for future use.

GRATED CHOCOLATE The simplest of all. Have the chocolate bar at room temperature and grate it finely or coarsely, as you wish. Always use a large piece of chocolate even if you only need a little, to save your fingers.

CHOPPED CHOCOLATE is often preferable to grated chocolate, as it provides something to bite on. Easiest to make with thin, continental bars. Chop the chocolate roughly with a large chopping knife on a board. It makes a marvellous children's tea-time treat thickly sprinkled on fresh bread and butter.

CHOCOLATE FLAKES Use thick chocolate bars, at room temperature. With a small, sharp kitchen knife or – best of all – a swivel-bladed potato peeler, shave off small or large flakes, which will curl as they drop.

CHOCOLATE CURLS take a little more time, but with

practice you can achieve beautiful, long, wafer-thin rolls of chocolate.

Melt some chocolate (see page 13) and, when smooth, spread about a dessertspoonful with a palette knife on a cold surface (marble is best; a laminated work surface will do). Spread it evenly and thinly into a strip not more than 8–10 cm (3–4 in) wide and ¼ cm (⅛ in) thick. Continue to smooth it with the palette knife until the surface becomes matt and the chocolate has set. Leave to cool for about one more minute – but it must not set hard.

Now take a large carving knife with a straight edge and, holding it with both hands at a very slight angle to your work surface, push it gently along into the chocolate, which will curl up ahead of the knife as it leaves the work surface. As soon as the chocolate breaks, set the 'curl' aside and begin again. Make more strips as needed.

Lift the curls up very carefully with the knife or, for truly magnificent specimens that are too large or fragile to lift by knife, use two toothpicks or skewers inserted one at either end.

CHOCOLATE LEAVES are very easy to make and never fail to impress. Choose some fresh green leaves in the garden – not too large, and they should have clear veins – rose leaves of different sizes are ideal. Wash them well and pat them quite dry with kitchen paper.

Melt some chocolate (see page 13) and, when smooth, spread a thin layer on the underside of each leaf with a knife, being careful to go right to the edge of the leaf but not on to the other side as this makes peeling difficult. Set on foil in a cool place to harden, then carefully peel off the leaf, starting from the stalk end.

CHOCOLATE SQUARES AND SHAPES Melt some chocolate (see page 13) and, when quite smooth, spread a thin, even layer, not more than $\frac{1}{4}$ cm ($\frac{1}{8}$ in) thick on foil or greaseproof paper, using a flexible palette knife.

When the surface of the chocolate becomes matt, mark out the shapes – squares, circles, moons, Christmas trees, flowers or whatever you wish – using a knife, or biscuit cutters, or working freehand. Leave till set hard, then peel off.

CHOCOLATE COFFEE BEANS make delicious and unusual decorations, especially for chocolate and coffee ices. Coffee lovers will devour them as confectionery.

Dip freshly roasted coffee beans in melted chocolate. Remove with spoon, fork, or sugar tongs and leave on foil to set.

CHOCOLATE FIGURES Make your own Father Christmas, Easter rabbits, eggs, chickens, ducks, elephants, cats' tongues and so on – there is no end to the pleasure to be had for adults and children of all ages from collecting metal chocolate moulds, new or antique (the older, the more finely detailed they tend to be). Modern plastic or rubberized moulds are also perfectly good but their range and detail is more limited.

Before 'casting' your chocolate, make sure the mould is scrupulously clean and dry: the best way is to polish the inside with a little cotton wool dipped in cornflour. Chill the mould.

After melting the chocolate (see page 13), stir it till smooth, then fill the mould, tap it on the table to eliminate air bubbles and leave to set at room temperature.

When the chocolate has set, put it in the freezer or freezing compartment of the refrigerator for 10–15 minutes, then

turn the chocolate out of the mould. It should come out quite easily, as the chocolate has contracted faster than the mould, but if necessary, give the mould a sharp tap.

If you are using a double-sided mould, peg or clip the two sides together. For a solid figure, pour in the chocolate up to the top, give it a good tap to expel any air bubbles and leave to set upside down, topping up if necessary with a little more chocolate after a few minutes.

To make a hollow figure, pour in some chocolate and turn the mould about for several minutes so that the sides become evenly and thickly coated all over. For larger figures, it may be advisable to do a second coat as soon as the first begins to set, as it can be difficult to remove the figures from the mould if they are too thin and fragile. Stand the figure right side up on a well-smoothed piece of foil and leave to set.

Remove pegs or clips before putting double-sided moulds into the freezer.

CHOCOLATE FRUIT may be used as decoration, or served as confectionery.

Prepare the fruit – cherries and firm strawberries look (and taste) lovely dipped in chocolate; carefully peeled orange segments, with all pith removed but the inner skin intact, are my particular favourite. Grapes, chunks of pineapple, slices of apple and pear and any citrus fruit may also be used.

For a special confection, dip the fruit in fondant first (see page 285) and leave to dry and harden before dipping in chocolate. These must be eaten very fresh.

CHOCOLATE FONDUE For chocoholics or children with stout stomachs only.

Melt 25 g (2 oz) chocolate with 1 tablespoon water, rum, brandy or liqueur per person (see page 13) in a heatproof serving dish.

Prepare a mixed platter of fresh fruit (see above) interspersed with plain biscuits or sponge fingers. You can also add a few crystallized or dried fruits.

Set the chocolate pot in the middle of the table and let everyone dip in a piece of fruit or biscuit, one at a time. Use fondue forks if possible.

You may need to reheat the chocolate gently half-way through, but if you use a fondue set with spirit flame, do not keep it on all the time as the chocolate will overheat and harden.

Use plain or milk chocolate, or a mixture of the two, or add the odd bar of special liqueur-flavoured or nut chocolate, such as Toblerone.

FROM TROPICAL COCOA TREE TO CHOCOLATE FACTORY

Archaeologists believe that the cocoa tree may be all of four thousand years old, and that it came from the Orinoco and Amazon regions of South America. Our first knowledge of the tree comes from the Aztecs, who, in their migrations through the sub-continent, probably brought the tree to Yucatan at around 600 AD.

The cocoa tree is a tropical plant that flourishes only in a narrow band round the centre of the earth, not more than 20° north or south of the equator. The Spanish established cocoa plantations throughout their Central and South American colonies, as well as in the Caribbean and the Philippines in the course of the sixteenth and seventeenth centuries. In the late seventeenth century, the Dutch took cocoa trees to Indonesia and Ceylon, and to the islands of Fernando Po and Sao Tome, off the coast of equatorial Africa. From here, cocoa was introduced to the Gold Coast in the late 1870s, and today Ghana and Nigeria are the world's leading cocoa growers, Brazil being the next largest producer.

The young cocoa tree is very delicate, and is usually planted in the shade of a larger, 'mother' tree. It takes at least three or four years for the tree to produce a crop, ten before it is fully mature, and after thirty years a cultivated tree has exhausted its economic usefulness, although trees have been known to live for more than two hundred years.

The trees can grow to a soaring height of 20 metres (60 feet), but are usually kept to no more than 8 metres (25 feet) to make harvesting easier.

The cocoa tree has large, glossy leaves, and five-petalled waxy white or pink blossoms that grow direct from the slender trunk and along the main branches of the tree, which is often also covered in lichen, moss and tiny wild orchids.

These blossoms, which flower all the year round, grow

'Early chocolate factory'

into large, rough-textured pods, 20–25 cm (8–10 in) long and 7–10 cm (3–4 in) wide, turning from green to yellow to russet brown, when they are ready for harvesting. Although the trees produce flowers and pods all year round, there are generally two major harvesting periods.

The pods are carefully cut off the tree by experienced pickers, who use small *machetes* for the lower pods and a special curved blade, that looks like a hand with outstretched thumb, attached to a long handle, for those that grow higher up the tree. Care must be taken not to damage the delicate young blossom that may be just next to the mature pods.

The pods are carried to a central area, where, with one blow of a *machete*, they are split open and the beans (between twenty and fifty per pod), together with the whitish pulp in which they are embedded, are scooped out.

The beans are left on the ground in great piles to ferment for between two and nine days, in order to remove the raw bitter taste and develop essential oils. Thereafter they must be dried off – in the sun in hot dry climates, or in long drying sheds in moist conditions. The beans have now lost about half their original weight, and are ready for shipping.

When the beans arrive at the factory, they are first of all sorted and blended. Broadly speaking there are two main types of beans – the *criollo*, from Central and South America, which is the Rolls-Royce of beans, very expensive, but with the finest and most concentrated flavour; and the *forastero*, which comes mostly from West Africa and Brazil, thicker-skinned and with a less delicate flavour, but which makes up the bulk of the world's production. There are also many hybrids that have their own special flavour. Every chocolate manufacturer blends his beans according to his particular secret formula.

The beans, once cleaned, sorted and blended, are then roasted – another highly delicate procedure, individual to each manufacturer, that relies on fine judgement, or a high degree of mechanization, depending on the size of the factory. The characteristic chocolate aroma (which is carried on the air for miles around) now begins to develop, and the beans turn a dark, rich brown.

After roasting, the beans are cracked to remove the shells and the tiny 'nibs' of which each bean consists are exposed, while the husks and the bitter-tasting root germ are winnowed or fanned off.

The beans are now crushed between giant steel rollers. This breaks down the cell walls of the nibs, reducing them to a paste and releasing the fat, or cocoa butter, while the heat that is generated by the friction melts down the cocoa butter – and the result is a thick, dark brown paste known as chocolate liquor. This sets on cooling and can be used as unsweetened cooking chocolate.

At this point, we come to the parting of the ways.

The chocolate liquor may now be fed through giant presses, which will extract 30 per cent or more cocoa butter, leaving a pure cocoa powder which will be crushed, milled and finely sifted before being marketed.

The other road leads to chocolate and, for the visitor to the modern chocolate factory, into the realms of pure fantasy.

The chocolate liquor is blended with additional cocoa butter, sugar, flavouring such as vanilla, and – if milk chocolate is to be made – with dried milk.

The resultant chocolate paste now goes through a rolling procedure, where it is passed through a series of vertically mounted steel rollers, which are rotating in opposite directions, each one faster than the previous one and at ever decreasing distances from each other. A modern refining machine can process up to 900 kg (2,000 lb) of chocolate paste per hour. The chocolate paste is fed ever upwards, until it reaches the top where it has become a very fine, flaky powder that is scraped off the top roller by a fixed blade. And still it tastes gritty.

Now comes the conching, an updated version of the process discovered by Rodolphe Lindt in 1880, so-called after the original shell-shaped vats used for the process. The chocolate is heated in giant vats (the most modern ones are enclosed, but there are still many where you can see this heaving sea of chocolate) and giant rollers move slowly up and down (or round and round in the modern, circular ones) constantly introducing a little air into the mass as they go, until the tiny particles have polished each other, and a soft film of cocoa butter has formed round each one (even more cocoa butter may be added at some stage), so that the result is truly a chocolate that is meltingly smooth. This may take anything from two to four days.

Now, after carefully reducing the temperature, or 'tempering', the chocolate is ready to be poured – another sight out of fairyland. Streams of liquid chocolate issue out of gleaming machinery at minutely controlled speeds and quantities into metal moulds that pass through on conveyor belts. Once filled, the moulds go on their way on vibrating belts, to send up any air bubbles in the chocolate, into cooling chambers, and then the chocolate is automatically turned out and passed on to the mechanized wrapping machines.

CHAPTER
8

DRINKS

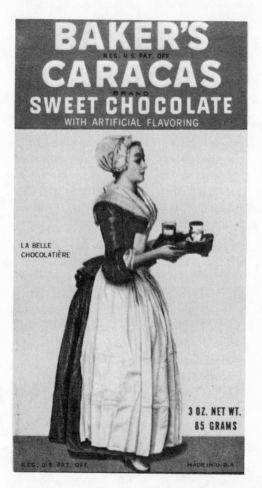

BAKER'S
REG. U.S. PAT. OFF.
CARACAS
BRAND
SWEET CHOCOLATE
WITH ARTIFICIAL FLAVORING

LA BELLE
CHOCOLATIÈRE

3 OZ. NET WT.
85 GRAMS

REG. U.S. PAT. OFF.   MADE IN U.S.A.

Generations of Americans are familiar with the painting of '*La Belle Choco-latière*', used as a trade mark by Baker's. It is a portrait of Anna Baltauf, who met her husband, Prince Dietrichstein, while working in a Viennese chocolate house. Prince Dietrichstein liked the new drink and came to love the girl who served it. As a wedding gift he had her painted by Liotard, but for this portrait he insisted that she pose in the chocolate server's dress she wore the day she met her Prince Charming

ICED CHOCOLATE

A delicious tea-time drink for a hot day. Keep a quantity of the basic syrup ready in the refrigerator, so that you can serve iced chocolate at short notice throughout the summer.

300 ML (½ PINT) WATER
225 G (8 OZ) SUGAR
50 G (2 OZ) COCOA POWDER
I HEAPED TEASPOON INSTANT COFFEE POWDER
(OPTIONAL)
MILK

To make the basic syrup, bring the sugar and water to the boil and boil briskly for 3 minutes. Add the cocoa and coffee and whisk over moderate heat until quite smooth. Leave to cool, then refrigerate.

To make iced chocolate drinks, blend the chilled syrup with cold milk, roughly in the proportion of I glass syrup to 4 glasses milk (more or less according to taste). Stir well, or mix in a blender, and pour into chilled glasses, over one or two ice cubes in each glass.

VARIATION: To make CHOCOLATE LIÉGEOIS serve the iced chocolate as above in tall, well-chilled glasses, float a scoopful of chocolate or vanilla ice cream on each glass, top with a good dollop of lightly whipped, lightly sweetened cream and sprinkle with a little cocoa.

Serve with drinking straws (and, as they do in some elegant French cafés, with a little paper umbrella perched on top!).

HOT DRINKING CHOCOLATE

Very rich, excellent for cold nights or après-ski.

You can give everyone a stick of cinnamon with which to stir their chocolate, which gives it just a subtle hint of cinnamon flavour. For stronger flavouring see the Spanish Drinking Chocolate below.

600 ML (1 PINT) MILK
100 G (3½ OZ) PLAIN OR BITTER CHOCOLATE
SUGAR (OPTIONAL)
¼ PINT WHIPPING CREAM (OPTIONAL)
COCOA POWDER (OPTIONAL)

Heat the milk, then add the chocolate and stir until the chocolate has melted.

Bring to simmering point and whisk over steady heat for at least 3 minutes, preferably using a wooden *molinet* (see page 111). Taste for sweetness and add a little sugar if you wish.

Pour very hot and frothing into cups or mugs. You can top each serving with a dollop of lightly whipped cream, sprinkled with a little cocoa.

VARIATION: To make a really rich SPANISH DRINKING CHOCOLATE, stir in ¼ teaspoon of ground cloves and ½ teaspoon of ground cinnamon. Whisk to a froth, then whisk in 1 egg yolk just before serving.

An eighteenth-century chocolate pot belonging to Marie Leczinska

AMBROSIAL COFFEE

A heavenly after-dinner drink. The additions must be very subtle, barely discernible in themselves but adding to the flavour of the coffee, which should be finely ground and, if possible, include some mocha beans.

VERY STRONG AFTER-DINNER COFFEE
BITTER CHOCOLATE
BRANDY
DOUBLE CREAM

Make your coffee very strong and very hot.

Warm the coffee cups and put one small square of chocolate in each.

Pour on the coffee, add a bare half-teaspoon of brandy, and pour on the cream over the back of a teaspoon, to float in a thick layer on top.

Serve without stirring – the chocolate will gradually melt into the coffee as you drink.

HAPPY MARRIAGE

Just as the title implies, a happy marriage between chocolate and coffee, all the more exciting for the fillip of a dash of brandy.

600 ML (I PINT) HOT DRINKING CHOCOLATE (SEE RECIPE ON PAGE 308)

300 ML ($\frac{1}{2}$ PINT) VERY STRONG, FRESHLY MADE BLACK
   COFFEE
1 COFFEE CUP OF BRANDY (OPTIONAL)
150 ML ($\frac{1}{4}$ PINT) WHIPPING CREAM

Combine the coffee with the drinking chocolate and bring
to just below boiling point.

Remove from the heat and add the brandy.

Serve with a dollop of lightly whipped cream floating on
each cup.

CHOCOLATE GROG

A powerful drink, adapted from an eighteenth-century naval
grog, which was a favourite drink of the great actor, David
Garrick. It was served at a celebration held in his honour on
the bicentenary of his death, in 1979, at London's Garrick
Club.

125 G (4 OZ) SUGAR
300 ML ($\frac{1}{2}$ PINT) WATER
25 G (1 OZ) COCOA
2 LARGE STICKS CINNAMON OR 1 GOOD TEASPOON
   GROUND CINNAMON
300 ML ($\frac{1}{2}$ PINT) MILK
75 ML ($\frac{1}{8}$ PINT) DARK RUM

Bring the sugar and water to the boil and boil briskly for 3
minutes. Add the cocoa, stir until smooth, then add the
cinnamon, cover and leave to infuse.

Bring the milk to the boil, strain in the syrup and bring
back to the boil. Remove from the heat, add the rum and
serve very hot.

MONTEZUMA

Don't be fooled by the high milk content – this is a very potent drink, the summer counterpart of chocolate grog. Serve at the end of a summer evening party.

600 ML (1 PINT) MILK
75 G (3 OZ) PLAIN OR BITTER CHOCOLATE
PINCH OF ALLSPICE
PINCH OF GINGER
1 TABLESPOON HONEY
75 ML ($\frac{1}{8}$ PINT) RUM
LIQUEUR GLASS OF EAU DE VIE DE MARC OR BRANDY
GRATED RIND OF $\frac{1}{2}$ LEMON

Heat the milk gently together with the chocolate, spices and honey, and stir until the chocolate has melted and the mixture is smooth. Leave to cool.

Pour the milk into a blender glass or a cocktail shaker, add remaining ingredients and blend or shake well.

Refrigerate and blend or shake again before serving.

CHOCOLATE COCKTAILS

Crème de cacao, a distillate of cocoa beans, is the most popular of the chocolate liqueurs. It can be either colourless or a dark, transparent brown, and is used as the dominant flavour in a number of cocktails. Here, for the brave, is a selection, using roughly equal quantities of each ingredient, but these may be varied according to taste.

Alexander
DRY GIN
CRÈME DE CACAO
CREAM

Nureyev
VODKA
COLOURLESS CRÈME DE CACAO

Pavlova
VODKA
CRÈME DE CACAO
CREAM

Puskin
VODKA
GIN
CRÈME DE CACAO

Crow
WHISKY OR BOURBON
CRÈME DE CACAO
DASH OF ORANGE BITTERS

Monseigneur Takes His Chocolate

Monseigneur, one of the great lords in power at the Court, held his fortnightly reception in his grand hotel in Paris. Monseigneur was in his inner room, his sanctuary of sanctuaries, the Holiest of Holiests to the crowd of worshippers in the suite of rooms without. Monseigneur was about to take his chocolate. Monseigneur could swallow a great many things with ease, and was by some few sullen minds supposed to be rather rapidly swallowing France; but his morning's chocolate could not so much as get into the throat of Monseigneur, without the aid of four strong men besides the Cook.

Yes. It took four men, all four a-blaze with gorgeous decoration, and the Chief of them unable to exist with fewer than two gold watches in his pocket, emulative of the noble and chaste fashion set by Monseigneur, to conduct the happy chocolate to Monseigneur's lips. One lacquey carried the chocolate-pot into the sacred presence; a second, milled and frothed the chocolate with the little instrument he bore for that function; a third, presented the favoured napkin; a fourth (he of the two gold watches), poured the chocolate out. It was impossible for Monseigneur to dispense with one of these attendants on the chocolate and hold his high place under the admiring Heavens. Deep would have been the blot upon his escutcheon if his chocolate had been ignobly waited on by only three men; he must have died of two.

FROM *A Tale of Two Cities* by Charles Dickens

Opposite chocolate pot with a characteristic handle at right angles to the spout. Madame de Pompadour was the first to commission a china chocolate service from the Sèvres factory.

EPILOGUE

On Christmas Eve, 1978, readers of London's Observer *were treated to the following prose poem, 'My Sweet Days to Christmas', in praise of chocolate. Many chocolate addicts indulge their passions only in the privacy of their closet. Gillian Widdicombe is delightfully candid about her ardent enthusiasm, eclectic in her taste and also knows a lot of chocolate lore.*

On the First Day of Christmas my truelove will give me a fresh cream Leonardis truffle.
It will melt upon my tongue (a luxury, a fantasy, an idyll) because this uncooked mix of fresh cream, butter and cocoa has the lowest melting point of all chocolate confectionery. Even on a knee-cap, between two toes, or in the ear, the same expensive fantasy would melt itself into the same perfect idyll. Yes, expensive! However, they're so rich that just one poetic mouthful is enough to obliterate prosaic memories of turkey.

On the Second Day my truelove will serve me a Mars Bar upon a silver salver.
The idea is not entirely original. According to legend, every day at Mars (which is still a family-owned company) the Mars brothers sample yesterday's bars from a silver salver. In fact, the chrome tray was recently replaced by a big plastic basket from which all executives in this most democratic of the big chocolate companies may chew daily.
    Chew bars were always the Mars speciality, thanks to Forrest

Mars, a Yale-educated industrial engineer, son of the Chicago confectioner who invented Milky Way in 1923.

'This company isn't big enough for both of us,' said Mars senior. 'Here's $5,000 and the recipe for Milky Way. Go abroad, son, and start your own company.'

Young Mars settled in Slough, and started his chew bars in 1932. During 1978, in the UK alone, more than 600 million Mars Bars will have been chewed. Have I eaten ten Mars Bars this year? Have you? If not, somebody is chewing for me and you.

Mars guard their recipes with almost paranoid secrecy. Indeed, Mars are regarded as something of a secret society by their two principal competitors, Rowntree and Cadbury.

Legends abound as to the uses of Mars Bars. The Rolling Stones were said to employ them as phallic symbols. Olympic trainers, before the advent of steroids, were said to feed their broods on a protein diet throughout the training period, then give them a Mars Bar on the big day. ZOOM!

On the Third Day of Christmas my truelove will treat me as a gourmet (connoisseur) rather than gourmand (glutton). An exquisite box of hand-made Favourites from Fortnum & Mason.
If there is an ultimate quality, an Elysian factory, or just one last example of the tiny old-fashioned, superfine chocolate maker it is here, at F & M in Piccadilly.

Here the very air is yummy, untainted by the sticky odour that permeates a big, modern chocolate factory. Here fondant centres are blobbed by hand into soft holes pressed in trays of loose starch, allowing a natural set over twenty-four hours; the modern way is to use rubber moulds, in which the fondant can be solidified in a few minutes. Here peppermint centres are made with precious drops from numbered bottles of Mitcham mint. Mitcham is not, I learn, just a couple of roundabouts between London and Croydon: it produces the finest mint oil in the world, the quantity being very small because the liquid must be distilled twice and matured for at least four years.

Here the fondant base is stiffer than usual, so that fresh fruit juices and canned fruit pulp may be used. Each year over thirty 2-cwt barrels of young baby stem ginger, called Chun Chun, are specially imported from China; and 500 lb of Morello cherries, ordered directly from one Kent grower, sit in oak casks of brandy for a full year before they may receive their chocolate coating. Here all chocolates are hand-dipped – an art generally eclipsed not only by technology but by the Public Health Inspector.

On the Fourth Day my truelove will remind me that there is always an exception to the rule. We shall crunch and chew our way through the new Double Decker from Cadbury.

The rule is that the number of things you can do with chocolate and sugar is quite limited, and most of them were discovered before 1939. However, during the early 1970s, the big three made an expensive effort to create new products, to revive the spirit of the 1930s. Since 1970, Mars, Cadbury and Rowntree have marketed forty-four new chocolate lines between them. Most flopped so badly that over thirty were soon withdrawn.

All sorts of new concoctions of the old ingredients were made at Bournville, the Cadbury factory near Birmingham. Remember Amazin Raisin ...? Whistler ...? Aztec? Rumba? No.

Up in York, Rowntree Mackintosh were pleased as punch, for a while, because they invented a new Mint Cracknel which, technologically, was very clever, spinning the pulled sugar centre by a process adapted from nylon manufacture. Alas, that didn't stick with the public either.

Was it, then, a little old lady who saved the day by posting her own recipe to Mr Cadbury? No. Mass production means chemistry, not cookery.

Market research led Cadbury to try a new texture rather than yet another mixture. A double unit: one soft layer, of nougatine with a slight coffee flavour; one crisp layer, of crushed cereals. Result, a very bland flavour.

Which conformed to the food industry's best-known maxim.

That in order to appeal to as many millions as possible, the product becomes increasingly bland. (It's not how many people you attract, it's how many you do not offend.)

Cadbury have sold 160 million Double Deckers in 1978, the first year of national distribution. (TV helps, of course.) That's three for you, three for me … But this is nothing compared with their Creme Egg statistics. Between Christmas and Easter, they will sell 200 million egg-sized fondant-filled horrors, the sickliest thing you can buy for (around) 10p. Four each, by Easter? I don't eat Creme Eggs. Nobody I know eats Creme Eggs. So who is going to kill themselves with all our Creme Eggs before Easter?

On Day Five my truelove will further instruct me on the story of Rowntree versus Cadbury. He will give me a Yorkie.
Cadbury started serious production with the Dairy Milk solid bars in 1905; Bournville, their plain bar, was added in 1910; Fruit and Nut in 1921. It was a very comfortable market, until cocoa prices rose. Then, instead of increasing their prices, they reduced the thickness of the moulded bars. They forgot, or perhaps never realized, that milk chocolate doesn't taste very chocolaty when the bar is thin.

Rowntree barged in. They had not done an ordinary solid milk chocolate block for many years, and they did not expect to knock out such a time-honoured winner as Dairy Milk. (After all, national taste is demonstrably formed by one kind of chocolate flavour. For the Americans it is the Hershey Bar, a stronger, coarser flavour; for the other Europeans it is still the smoother, luxurious blend of the classic Swiss makers; for the British, it is Cadbury's Dairy Milk.) Rowntree tried various recipes, and eventually settled on a rather sweeter sort of chocolate similar to their covering for Rollo. They also considered the market position of the new product. Yes, a thick, narrow bar similar in size to a filled bar; solid milk chocolate, but able to be snapped into pieces in case a covetous friend is at the bus stop with you. TV advertising. Yorkie soared. Cadbury re-

covered face by relaunching Dairy Milk, restoring the thickness
and raising the price.

*On the Sixth Day of Christmas my truelove will behave like the superior
English gentleman I wish he were throughout the year. He will give me
a Boîte Blanche from Charbonnel et Walker of Bond Street.*
When I open the 5 lb box, gold-covered chocolate letters will spell
out 'GILLIAN WIDDICOMBE – I LOVE YOU.'
Charbonnel's special white boxes are round, so a long name needs
a lot of chockies to fill the centre: my truelove would find 'SUZY
WONG' cheaper.

To prove his love further he could order a selection of my
favourite centres. Charbonnel are famous for their personal
services. Once you've made one personal order, they record the
selection so that your secretary can just phone and say 'A pound
of the usual.'

It's not true, though, that Charbonnel are patronized only by
rich ladies. Their manager says 'It's surprising how many men like
rose and violet creams.' The Royal Family evidently shop here, the
Queen Mother being a sweet-toothed lady. Since Charbonnel's
characteristic flavours are rather strong (some say too sweet, even
sickly), I wonder whether she also tackles Creme Eggs occasionally.

*On the Seventh Day my truelove will declare that I have been over-eating
between meals. Today he will administer a single specimen of the post-
prandial classic, the Bendicks Bittermint.*
Beware of imitations. The classic Bittermint is totally different
from the sweet, sticky wafer-like copies that TV viewers have been
lulled into regarding the perfect end to the posh dinner party. The
Bendicks Bittermint is a fat, filling object, its fondant centre firm
and strong, if no longer flavoured by the weed of Mitcham. It is
no longer hand-dipped, because Bendicks have found it preferable
to use the Kreuter enrober (good name to drop), which gives as
thick a coating because it performs a miraculous double dip. Most
people cannot tell the difference between hand-dipped and enrobed

chocolates. Secret tip: the base of the hand-dipped chocolate is usually thicker.

Once upon a time there was a Madame Charbonnel (a French lady encouraged by a Prince of Wales). Never a Mister Bendicks. But there was a Major Benson, who got together in a Mayfair backroom with a Captain Dickson, immediately after the First World War. Since last month Bendicks have been owned by Associated Biscuits. For ten years they have manufactured in a splendid modern factory on a trading estate between the M3 and Winchester. Next door is the local abattoir, outside which a lonely ram can be seen inviting flocks of sheep to slaughter.

On the Eighth Day, to Marks & Spencer.

The only snag about chocolates from Marks & Spencer is that the St Michael label on the dinner table may remind your guests of socks and sweaters. Bring out the silver salver and you can fool them altogether. You could even refer to St Michael's Mint Crisps as 'Bendicks, of course!' since these green-foiled delectables are made under contract in that computerized factory between the M3 and the abattoir. But there is a difference, in both mint and chocolate flavour, the M & S recipe being noticeably more bland.

On the Ninth Day, back to Harrods.

If I told you that the beautiful dark chocolate assortment sold as Harrods own brand was also made between the M3 and the abattoir, you might not believe me. Neither party will bless me for telling you, but it happens to be true. Harrods did have their own little chocolate factory, in the basement of the Knightsbridge store; but that closed, like the famous Harrods bakery.

Notwithstanding computer and the Kreuter enrober, Harrods swear that their recipes are the same as they always were. Certainly the Harrods touch survives the transfer: the lady who packs all assortment boxes leaving Bendicks gives the top chocolates a loving polish with a soft camelhair brush. Hand-polished chocolates!

On the Tenth Day, a token Smartie.
Ten thousand million Smarties are consumed in the UK annually. They pop off Rowntree's production line at the rate of 30,000 a minute.

On the Eleventh Day, I shall not be hungry.
But I may fantasize about a wholly synthetic chocolate recently invented in the US by Procter & Gamble.

On the Twelfth Day of Christmas my truelove will bid me tell him what I'd like for Christmas next year.
Not so silly as it seems. Charbonnel have a favourite customer who comes in every September to order two boxes for Valentine's day, half a year away. One for his wife? He leaves the shop sighing, 'Thank God that's over!'   (*Abridged.*)

★   ★   ★   ★   ★   ★   ★   ★   ★

'Monsieur,' Madame d'Arestel, Superior of the Convent of the Visitation at Belley, once said to me more than fifty years ago, 'whenever you want to have a really good cup of chocolate, make it the day before, in a porcelain coffee-pot, and let it set. The night's rest will concentrate it and give it a velvety quality which will make it better. Our good God cannot possibly take offence at this little refinement, since he himself is everything that is most perfect.'

(from J.-A. Brillat-Savarin, *Physiologie du goût, 1825*)

★   ★   ★   ★   ★   ★   ★   ★   ★

BIBLIOGRAPHY

Writing this book has been a two-fold pleasure: one has been the testing and tasting of recipes, the other the time spent browsing in libraries, searching out material for the historical sections. While not pretending that this is a scholarly work, I append nonetheless a list of the books that have been most helpful, from many of which I have quoted in the text, and from which the reader might also derive further enjoyment.

Aztecs of Mexico: G. C. Vaillant, Allen Lane, 1962

The Native Races of the Pacific States of North America: H. H. Bancroft, London, 1875

History of the New World: Girolamo Benzoni, published in Venice, 1565, translation published for the Hakluyt Society, 1857

The English-American, his Travail by Sea and Land, or A New Survey of the West Indies: Thomas Gage, 1648

Historia verdadera de la Conquista de la Nueva España: Bernal Díaz del Castillo, translated by J. M. Cohen, Penguin Books, 1963; Folio Society, 1976

Le Bon Usage du thé, du café et du chocolat pour la préservation et pour la guérison de maladies: M. de Blégny, Lyon, 1687

Le Parfait Limonadier ou la manière de préparer le thé, le caffé, le chocolat et autres liqueurs chaudes et froides: P. Masson, Limonadier, Paris, 1705

Amusements of Old London: Boulton, London, 1901

London Coffee Houses: Lillywhite, London, 1963

Victorians and Drink: Brian Harrison, Faber, 1971

Seltsame Frucht, Kakao: Wolf Mueller, Gordian, 1957

Das Buch über die Schokolade: Valerian Tornius, Leipzig, 1931

Curiosities of Literature: Isaac Disraeli, 1823

Cocoa, All About It, 'Historicus', London, 1892

As for cookery books, I have obviously browsed in and borrowed ideas here and there from too many to list, but the following have been invaluable:

Lenôtre's Desserts and Pastries: Gaston Lenôtre, Barron's, 1977

Lenôtre's Ice Creams and Candies: Gaston Lenôtre, Barron's, 1979

Backe nach Grundrezepten: Cornelia Kopp, Otto Beyer Verlag, 1933

Kochbuch für Drei: H. Lamprecht, Munich, 1922

Mastering the Art of French Cooking: Simone Beck, Louisette Bertholle, Julia Child, Cassell, 1963

From Julia Child's Kitchen: Julia Child, Jonathan Cape, 1978

The Viennese Pastry Cookbook: Lilly Joss Reich, Collier Macmillan, 1970

*   *   *   *   *   *   *   *   *

Perhaps 80 per cent of the world's population
have never eaten chocolate or drunk cocoa.

New York Times, Sunday, 25 February 1979

*   *   *   *   *   *   *   *   *

ACKNOWLEDGEMENTS

My first thanks must go to my family: to my husband for having the greedy idea for this book, to all of them for tireless eating, and most of all to my son Ben for patiently experimenting with the 'casting' of chocolate until he finally perfected the technique.

I am indebted to Alan Scholefield for his help with the historical section, and to Dr Leonard Beck, from the Rare Books Department of the Library of Congress in Washington, for gently guiding me in the very early stages of my quest.

The fraternity of cookery writers is enormously generous, and I am especially grateful to Elisabeth Lambert Ortiz and to Anne Willan for allowing me to browse among their books, and to Alan Davidson for valuable contacts and references.

Among the numerous chocolate factories I visited I particularly enjoyed my tour around the Van Leer factory, in Hoboken, guided by the founder's grandson Tad van Leer.

Finally, I am grateful to Debbie Campbell for so cheerfully coping with the typing.

Credit is due to Oxford University Press for permission to reproduce 'Chocolates', from *Caviare at the Funeral* by Louis Simpson, © Louis Simpson 1981; the *Observer* for permission to reproduce 'My Sweet Days to Christmas' by Gillian Widdicombe; Elisabeth Lambert Ortiz and Jill Norman Ltd for permission to reproduce Mole Poblano de Guajolote from *The Book of Latin American Cooking* by Elisabeth Lambert Ortiz; Elisabeth Ayrton and André Deutsch Ltd for permission to reproduce The Royal Recipe for Hare from *The Cookery of England* by Elisabeth Ayrton.

Art Institute of Chicago: frontispiece; Author's collection: 250, 257; BBC Hulton Picture Library: 6, 24, 38, 39, 44, 46, 51, 66, 115, 189, 194; Bettman Archive: 69, 146, 218, 300; Bildarchiv Preussischer Kulturbesitz: 263; Bodleian Library, John Johnson Collection: 14, 77, 105, 111, 157, 169, 171, 173, 183, 202, 207, 226, 254, 272, 297, 316; British Museum, photo John Freeman: 57, 138, 141, 142, 264, 325; Bruckman, F. E., *Relatio brevis historica – botanica medica de Avellana Mexicana, vulgo Cacao dicta*, Brunswick, 1728: 61; Cadbury Schweppes Ltd: 54, 118, 120, 122, 124, 131, 135, 148, 176, 212, 237, 252, 283, 291, 297; Mel Calman: 198; Photo Charmet: 22, 26, 42, 59, 72, 79, 81, 112, 187, 210, 214, 276; Courtauld Institute: 241; De Blegny, M., *Le Bon Usage du Thé, du Café et du Chocolat pour la Préservation et pour la Guérison de Maladies*: 298; Dufour, *Treatise on Coffee, Tea and Chocolate*, 1685: 14, 61; Photo Giraudon: 10, 185, 304, 309, 314; Mary Evans Picture Library: 35; Merseyside County Museums, Liverpool, Codex Féjerváry-Mayer (12014): 37; Prado, Madrid: L. E. Melendez 'Service à Chocolat': 10; Robert Opie Collection: 86, 88, 90, 125, 306; H. Roger Viollet; 84, 96, 108, 145, 152, 260, 266, 278, 286, 295; Rowntree Mackintosh Ltd: 92, 159, 230; Valerian Tornius, *Das Buch über die Schokolade*, 1931: 245; Van Nelle Confectionery Group: 164; Jim Wire: 216, 270.

Picture research by Susan Rose-Smith.

GENERAL INDEX

INDEX OF RECIPES